PRAISE FOR

MR. MEAN:
SAVING YOUR RELATIONSHIP FROM
THE IRRITABLE MALE SYNDROME

"Jed Diamond strips away the 'shield of armor,' revealing the naked truth about men's vulnerabilities at mid-life. This is the 'go to guide' every woman must have to save herself, understand and support her mate, and strengthen their marriage. Men will absolutely benefit from this treasure trove of solid information as well."

—Nancy Cetel, M.D., author of *Double Menopause: What To Do When Both You and Your Mate Go Through Hormonal Changes Together.*

"Watch out guys, Jed Diamond packs a mean punch. This is a wake-up call to everyone who thinks that it's only women who are mentally transitioning and transforming during mid-life. This book is terrific for women who want a heads up about what makes men tick, and for men who need to take themselves on and 'work it' to optimize their relationships."

—Pam M. Peeke, M.D., MPH, author of *Fight Fat after Forty, Body for Life for Women, and Fit to Live* and host of Discovery Health TV's *Could You Survive?*

"Jed Diamond is not inclined to give angry men a pass. He wants them to understand what they can do to deal with their irritability and anger—and he wants their partners to know what they need to do. If there is a Mr. Mean in your life—or a Mr. Mean looking at you in the mirror—this book is for you."

—Eric Maisel, PhD, author of *Brainstorm: Harnessing the Power* of *Productive Obsessions*

"A must read for women and for men who ʰ ⸱ the courage to see themselves through the eyes of their ⸱⸱⸱⸱⸱⸱ Mean cuts to the core of what is undermining ⸱⸱⸱⸱ ⸱⸱⸱⸱⸱ ʳ. It doesn't just help us understand thᵉ ⸱⸱⸱⸱⸱⸱⸱ ᵉ solutions that can save your marriᵉ⸱⸱

—John Gray, Ph.D., ⸱ ⸱ᵒm *Mars, Women Are From Venus*

"I love this book. I want to order one for every client I have. Finally, a book written for women about men by the world's leading expert on men's health. Dr. Diamond has spent close to a half a century as a psychotherapist helping men and the women who love them. Mr. Mean is the preeminent guide for women that answers the critical questions we have about how we can help ourselves, our men and our marriages. This is a book every woman must buy for herself and for every woman she cares about. It is a book that transcends gender and will be of huge value to men as well."

— Jackie Black, Ph.D., author of *Couples & Money: Cracking The Code To Ending the #1 Conflict In Marriage.*

"Jed Diamond has written the most compassionate guide for helping women and men heal their relationships now, and forever. It is the most accurate, practical, and immediately helpful book you can buy for yourself or someone you care about. I highly recommend it to women and the men they love."

—Pat Love, Ed.D., author, *The Truth About Love and Hot Monogamy*

"An insightful, well-written and compassionate book, written with the heart and wisdom of someone who has worked on the issue in himself, in his relationship and with patients."

—Warren Farrell, Ph.D., author of *Why Men Are the Way they Are, and Women Can't Hear What Men Don't Say*

"Jed Diamond is one of the wisest and bravest men writing today on the topic of male emotional and physical health. This book is useful and written with passion. It helps men look at their own changing lives and helps women understand their husbands and male friends. Jed Diamond's research is an important addition to men's work and the human journey of relationship building."

—Michael Gurian, Ph.D., author of *What Could He Be Thinking* and *Leadership and the Sexes.*

"Jed Diamond's lifetime of work in the area of men's health is unsurpassed. His latest book, Mr. Mean, illuminates the changes and accompanying challenges that often surface in a man's midlife. As importantly, Jed 'nets it out' and gives readers clear answers to specific questions succinctly and with compassion. Mr.

Mean is a must have guidebook for both men and women navigating mid-life waters. It is guaranteed to make for smoother sailing.

—Sharon Whiteley, former CEO of ThirdAge Inc. and author of *The Old Girls' Network.*

"I read this important work because I've loved everything else Jed has written. I ended up not being able to put it down because his powerful insights were not only helping me professionally, but personally as well. This is a ground-breaking work that will benefit both the professional therapist as well as the millions of men and women who must confront the 'irritable male syndrome' in their lives. This is a very, very important work."

—John Lee author of *The Anger Solution* and *The Flying Boy: Healing the Wounded Man*

"*Mr. Mean* is required reading for any woman in a relationship with a man. What a relief to find a book that finally explains the hidden thoughts and feelings of men who are secretly struggling to feel good about themselves. *Mr. Mean* explains the jumbled up feelings of men who are seething inside and provides a roadmap for the women who love them."

—Vikki Stark, M.S.W. Author of *Runaway Husbands: The Abandoned Wife's Guide to Recovery and* Renewal

"Dr. Diamond has given me insights into the profound mid-life challenges the man in my life is facing, along with practical advice on how to rescue our relationship from the negative impact of Irritable Male Syndrome. His book has helped me see that the 'curse' of IMS can be seen as a blessing, a chance to look closely at my own behaviors and life choices. It's given me the courage and tools to take action NOW to do more than improve my relationship with my husband. It's helped me figure out how to heal my relationship with myself, too!"

—Susan Walker, wife and mother

"For more than 40 years, therapist Jed Diamond's personal and professional life has revolved around helping men and women who love them. Now he offers advice for women bewildered by a male partner's irritability, anger, and withdrawal. He explains the reasons, the dynamics, and what she can do to help. Sound advice plus reader stories may help you save your marriage.

—Joan Price, author of *Better Than I Ever Expected: Straight Talk about Sex After Sixty*

"Today, 12,000 Baby Boomer men turned 50 and another 10,000 turned 60. Unprecedented aging of the male population, coupled with contemporary economic and social challenges, has created a crisis that many women must understand, confront and manage. Boomer men are searching for answers to complex challenges connected with male aging; some of these challenges foment anger and depression. Mr. Mean has substantial value for Boomer women who are trying to address significant and unpredictable changes in the men they love. This well-crafted, insightful book provides Boomer women and men with knowledge, encouragement and practical coping strategies. Jed Diamond's sensitivity to this life-stage passage is profound and uplifting.

—Brent Green, author of *Marketing to Leading-Edge Baby Boomers* and *The Boomer Future*

"*Mr.* Mean is a book that can be of vital interest to men and women of all ages, whether you are in a relationship or hoping to be. Dr. Diamond does an excellent job of helping women understand the men in their lives and also helps men better understand themselves."

— Isadora Alman, MFT author of *Bluebirds of Impossible Paradises: A Sexual Odyssey of the Seventies*

"Jed Diamond, author of superlative books relating to men and masculinity dating back over nearly three full decades, has produced an important and original book addressing a topic that to my knowledge has never before been treated in print. As usual with Dr. Jed, it is engaging to read and enlightening to learn from. It can help women learn about men and, at least as importantly, can help men learn about themselves."

—J. Steven Svoboda, co-author of *Does Feminism Discriminate Against Men?: A Debate*

"Women, this one's for you! For years Jed Diamond has been sharing his wisdom about Male Menopause and the Irritable Male Syndrome with men and the women who love them. When someone we care about is hurting, our first impulse is to do whatever we can to help them without regard to personal cost. Jed offers insight into why men sometimes behave badly while simultaneously encouraging women to practice good self-care. This kind of wisdom is long overdue. Mr. Mean is the perfect resource for women dealing with IMS."

—Judy Whelley, Ed.D., Educator, writer, and woman who's been there.

"Jed Diamond's book teaches women how to do two very important things: 1) develop profound empathy and understanding for the men they love, and 2) take responsibility for themselves in their relationships. Every woman who has been married for any length of time ought to read this book. Whether or not your man has IMS right now, you'll get incredibly valuable guidance on how to grow yourself and your relationship."

—Karen Jones, author of *Men Are Great*

Jed Diamond, Ph.D.

MR. MEAN:

SAVING YOUR RELATIONSHIP FROM THE IRRITABLE MALE SYNDROME

VOX NOVUS
A NUMINA PRESS BOOK
SAN RAFAEL, CALIFORNIA

Library of Congress Cataloging-in-Publication Data

Diamond, Jed, 1943-
 Mr. Mean : saving your relationship from the irritable male syn-drome / Jed Diamond.
     p. cm.
 ISBN 978-0-9842600-1-0
 1. Climacteric, Male. 2. Man-woman relationships. 3. Middle-aged men—Psychology. 4. Middle-aged men—Health and hygiene. I. Title.
 RC884.D523 2010
 306.7—dc22
                                    2010010642

Cover photograph © 2010 Jerri-Jo Idarius
Cover design © 2010 Vikyan Design

An e-book edition of *MR. MEAN: Saving Your Relationship from the Irritable Male Syndrome* is available on www.scribd.com

Printed in U.S.A.

ALSO BY JED DIAMOND

Male vs. Female Depression: Why Men Act Out and Women Act In

The Irritable Male Syndrome: Understanding and Managing the 4 Key Causes of Aggression and Depression

The Whole Man Program: Reinvigorating Your Body, Mind, and Spirit After 40

Surviving Male Menopause: A Guide for Women and Men

Male Menopause

The Warrior's Journey Home: Healing Men, Healing the Planet

Looking for Love in All the Wrong Places: Overcoming Romantic and Sexual Addictions

Inside Out: Becoming My Own Man

ACKNOWLEDGMENTS

This book is dedicated to my wife, Carlin, to our children, and to all the men, women, and children whose lives have been affected by the Irritable Male Syndrome. May this book be a source of healing for us all.

TABLE OF CONTENTS

Introduction:
Why I Wrote This Book For You!

Shortly after *The Irritable Male Syndrome* was published in 2004, I began to get letters from women all over the world who recognized themselves and the men in their lives in the stories I recounted in the book. This is typical of many I received:

"Well, I'm finding the book very helpful. I'm almost through it. Jesus, it must be very hard to be a man. I've found a new empathy for my husband, Steven, and also gained a greater understanding of what my son is going through, as he too is irritable from time to time. Anyway, it's much better for me, I'm not taking any of it personally, at the moment, and Steven's starting to make some lifestyle changes to improve his health, which I am sure will help his hormone levels and thus his mood. Just thought you should hear the good stuff! KL"

While it was great hearing from people who had been helped by the book, it would break my heart to hear from those who learned about the book too late to save their relationship.

"I wish I had learned about your book a year ago. It might have saved our marriage. His personality began to change from my funny, loving Dr. Jekyll into an angry, resentful, and controlling Mr. Hyde. He grew increasingly angry with me and seemed to withdraw from our marriage spending most of the time when he got home from work, including dinner time, in his home office or at the neighborhood bars. Simultaneously, he was constantly criticizing me for the things he once used to compliment me on.

When I expressed a desire to go back to school and then work, he said that he didn't understand why I couldn't be happy staying home. Since it was an every day exercise in futility, I just couldn't be happy staying home, especially if I was going to be slapped in the face with a bunch of criticism and anger.

"I hope others can get help before it's too late. JL."

The letters that energized me the most were the ones from women in crisis who were struggling to keep their heads above water trying to rescue their relationship.

"Last month a man came home from work with my husband's face but he did not act at all like the man I married. I've known this man for 30 years, married 22 of them and have never met this guy before. Angry, nasty, and cruel are just a few words to describe him. He used to be the most upbeat, happy person I knew. Now he's gone from Mr. Nice to Mr. Mean. In spite of how he treats me I still love my husband and want to save our marriage. Please, can you help me? MK"

All the women who wrote me wanted more information about what they could do to help themselves, help their relationship, and help their man. Their questions were diverse and covered a wide range of topics. How do I get through to him when he blames me for everything? Why has he changed? Does he have Irritable Male Syndrome? How do I take care of myself? What can I do to help him? How can I save our relationship?

If you're reading this book you know how devastating Irritable Male Syndrome can be. It can destroy a good relationship. It can cause you to question your sanity. It can turn a man who swore everlasting love and devotion into a man who seems angry and irritated a great deal of the time and sees you as the "enemy."

Most women are trained, from birth, to take care of others. When the man in their lives begins to act mean, they do everything they can to try and help him. But for many, the more they try and help him, the angrier and more abusive he becomes. One thing I've learned about working with IMS males, it is this:

The only way you can help him is to help yourself.

This book will help you understand what is really going on with him when he acts like "Mr. Mean." It will help you overcome your tendency to blame yourself for his bad behavior. You will also learn to stand up to him when he insists that you are the cause of his unhappiness. Finally, you will be given the tools to help him break through his denial so that you will both be on the same side and can confront the Irritable Male Syndrome together.

Although the book is directed at women, it will also be of interest to men. Many gay men have told me that they are having similar problems with irritability and anger with their partners. Many straight men are breaking through their denial and recognizing that they have gone from Mr. Nice to Mr. Mean and are ready to see things from a woman's perspective.

Much has changed since *The Irritable Male Syndrome* was first published in 2004. More people know about IMS and are reaching out for help. However, the world has become an increasingly stressful place to live and more people are suffering from IMS. Economic implosion, major earthquakes, job losses, global warming, war and the threats of more war, rising food prices, increasing levels of depression—are just a few of the challenges that are causing more of us to become frightened, frustrated, irritable, and angry.

But there are also signs of positive change. In tough times many people are realizing the importance of a good relationship. Instead of walking away, they want to stay and work things out. They recognize that there are reasons why men are becoming more irritable and angry, and they want more effective tools to improve their lives.

My wife and I have been together for 30 years. We have five grown children and twelve grandchildren. We've experienced our own struggles with IMS and managed to come through with our relationship stronger and more loving than ever. I want to share what we've learned, and what I've discovered from the thousands of people who have counseled with me.

Together we can learn how to improve ourselves, deepen our relationships, and help preserve life on this fragile planet we all share. I look forward to your reading this book, and I'd like to hear from you.

Note: A few things you need to know to get the most out of the book.

There are a number of ways you can read this book. You can go from start to finish. Or you can go immediately to those chapters that are of most concern to you. I do recommend that everyone begin by reading chapters 1, 2, and 3. They contain information you'll want to know now. Although each chapter addresses a specific question, you'll find that the information and answers from one chapter will be quite helpful to you as you address issues from other chapters. I've repeated some important information in more than one place to be sure you don't miss it. At the end of each chapter, there is a place for you to write down your experiences. You can do so in the book or separately.

About "men" and "women": I will talk in the book about things men and women feel and do. Please be aware that I don't mean *all* men are this way or *all* women are that way. These should be understood as tendencies or averages. We know, for instance, when we say, "men are taller than women," that this is true *on average*. I'm aware every day that at 5 feet 5 inches tall, there are many women who are taller than I am. Although what I say about men and women will fit for most of you, some of you will find that you identify more with things said about the other sex.

Let me know what was helpful to you in the book, what you learned, and any questions you may have.

Best wishes for a better tomorrow.

Jed Diamond

Contact me: Jed@MenAlive.com
If you need help now, want more information about my work, or wish to receive my free e-newsletter, go to www.MenAlive.com

Part 1:

Confronting the Crisis

Chapter 1: My Man Has Changed From "Mr. Nice" to "Mr. Mean". What Is Going On?

Dear Dr. Diamond,

For about a year now (it could be even longer, it's hard to know exactly), I have gradually felt my husband of 22 years pulling away for me and our family. He has become more sullen, angry, and moody. His general life energy is down and his sex drive has really dropped off.

Recently he has begun venting to anyone who will listen about how horrible we all are. He is particularly hard on our 19-year-old son, Mark. It's so surprising because our son has always been super industrious and competent. My husband has always shared my view that Mark is one of the hardest working kids we know. But all of a sudden that has all changed. Mark still works from 6:30 AM until 4:30 PM everyday, but now his Dad accuses him of being unmotivated, lazy, and anything else he can think to say that is negative.

The thing that bothers me the most is how unaffectionate he has become. I don't even get the hugs and affection like I did in the past and when he does touch me, I feel grabbed rather than caressed. My husband used to be the most positive, upbeat, funny person I knew. Now it's like living with an angry brick! I'm totally confused. What's going on? Can you help us? Thank you, LT.

I've been a psychotherapist specializing in men's health issues for more than 40 years. I first heard about guys who had changed from "Mr. Nice" to "Mr. Mean" when I was doing research for my books on Male Menopause between 1995 and 1997. Most all of the attention had been focused on erectile dysfunction and low libido in men over 40. When interviewing men and women I found them more often talking about male irritability, anger, and withdrawal. LT captures the essence of what is going on with the men when she says *"Now it's like living with an angry brick!"*

The men seem angry, but it's a cold, hard anger that is devoid of real passion. Not only is their sexuality compromised, but their life-energy is running dangerously low. These men are dying inside and their irritability, anger, and withdrawal are anguished cries for help. I know because I was one of those guys.

HEALER, HEAL THYSELF

I've always known that I became a psychotherapist as a way to heal my own wounds as much as to help others. But even after many years as a counselor, I was not prepared when Irritable Male Syndrome (IMS) came into our lives. For Carlin and me, IMS nearly destroyed our marriage. Here's how I described what happened:

After many years of being in a wonderful marriage, something seemed to be eating at the very roots of our joy and commitment. It seemed like Carlin had become less supportive of me. She would do things that irritated me, like showing up late for an engagement. I would react with anger and she would withdraw, which usually made me angrier.

I felt I was working my butt off and not getting much appreciation for my efforts. As I was getting older I thought I would be able to work less and have more time to enjoy life. But somehow it wasn't happening. Rather than cutting back on work, I was doing even more. I told myself it was so we'd have more money to do the things we both wanted to do. The truth was, I had spent so much of my life on the run, winning races, reaching for success, I didn't know how to slow down or shift gears.

I knew my irritation and anger were excessive, but I just couldn't shake the thought that I deserved more and Carlin was going out of her way to frustrate me. "Of course I'm angry," I would fume. "*Who wouldn't be angry when someone is hitting you in the head with a two-by-four.*"

Carlin, of course, saw things differently. Here's how she described her confusion:

The things most troubling about Jed are his rapid mood changes. He's angry, accusing, argumentative and blaming one moment and the next moment he is buying me flowers, cards, and leaving me loving notes. He'll change in an hour from looking daggers at me to being all smiles and enthusiasm.

He gets frustrated, red in the face, insists that we have to talk, then cuts me off when he judges I have said something offensive to him. I become frozen inside, feeling that no matter what I do or say, it will be "wrong" for him. The intensity and the coldness in his eyes scare me at these times. I usually shut down and it takes a lot of time for me to return to an open feeling towards him. My desire, trust, and joy in being together have suffered greatly."

Though we both knew we needed help, we didn't know how to reach out for it. This might seem strange for a therapist to say. But I've found healers are not immune to having problems and we often are so convinced that we have the answers, we are reluctant to admit that we can't fix the problem ourselves.

After living with the confusion, frustration and pain for a number of years, we finally went to see a doctor. Well, actually, it took us a long time to find the right doctor for us. Most of the people we sought out didn't really understand what we were experiencing. We didn't have words to adequately describe what was going on with us.

One of the most insightful descriptions of what I was feeling was given by Kay Redfield Jamison, herself a well-known researcher and therapist. In her exceptionally fine book, *An Unquiet Mind*, she talked openly about her own struggles with mental illness and her road to recovery.

Hers were the first words that captured what I had been experiencing over the past 5 years.

"You're irritable and paranoid and humorless and lifeless and critical and demanding and no reassurance is ever enough. You're frightened, and you're frightening, and 'you're not at all like yourself but will be soon,' but you know you won't."

I felt like someone truly understood me. I thought, "If she can get help for herself and write about it in a way that can help others, so can I." After looking around and asking a lot of questions, we did find a therapist who understood and could help. That was in April 1998. What you will learn in this book is based on our own experiences, my clinical research, and the feedback I've received from thousands of men and women who were helped by reading my book, *The Irritable Male Syndrome: Understanding and Managing the 4 Key Causes of Aggression and Depression.* Here are the first insights developed about Irritable Male Syndrome:

- Though it can start out mild, it can become extremely serious.
- It can eat away at a family like a deadly cancer.
- Though the mood changes may be the most obvious sign, it is quite complex.
- The people living with an IMS male often receive the brunt of his acting out.
- The symptoms are similar to andropause (male menopause), but it is not limited to middle-aged men.
- The symptoms are also related to male-type depression which is often expressed through irritability rather than sadness.
- Though it is most noticeable in men going through major transitions such as adolescence or mid-life, it can occur at any age.
- At first the man himself may be quite unaware that anything is wrong.
- As the problem progresses, he may realize that something is wrong, but blames the problem on something or someone else.
- The earlier it is recognized and addressed, the easier it is to treat.
- Getting through to a man suffering from IMS can seem impossible at times, but all men can be helped.
- Often the woman is trying to help, but doing things that make the problem worse.
- Whether caught at earlier or later stages, there is always hope for men with IMS.
- Families can survive. Couples can regain the intimacy and love that they've lost.
- We need to understand that this is a newly recognized disorder. There is much we do not know. I'm learning along with my clients. Scientific studies are just beginning to take place.
- As a therapist who has been working with men and couples for many years, and a man who is dealing with IMS in his own life, I know we can't wait until all the information is available

before we share what we do know with the people who are suffering.

In the spirit of explorers, let's move ahead. I remember the words from an old song from the sixties: "Something's happening here. What it is ain't exactly clear." It is my hope that we can begin to get some clarity on the nature of Irritable Male Syndrome and how to best treat it.

Here's your chance to write down some things about your situation. In the following space describe changes going on with the man in your life. List the main concerns that you have. How have his changes impacted your life?

NOTES

NOTES

Chapter 2: Why Do I Need to Save Myself Before I Can Rescue the Relationship?

Dear Dr. Jed,

I read your book and I believe my husband is suffering from irritable male syndrome and male-type depression. He's angry all the time and blames me for everything that is wrong. He calls me names, yells at me, looks at me with such hatred, I want to disappear. He's never hit me, but I'm afraid of him. He totally denies that there are any problems with him. When he gets mad he calls me a bitch and a lot worse and tells me I'm crazy and should be hospitalized.

His beliefs get reinforced by his family who also denies that there is anything wrong with him, though they've seen how angry and abusive he can be. They tell me that he wasn't depressed before he married me so it must be me that is the problem.

I love my husband with all my heart and I want to get him the help he needs. I know that he must be suffering. If he would just acknowledge the problem I'm sure we could work things out. Can you help me get through to him? SL.

I get calls and e-mails regularly from women who are sure their partner is suffering from irritable male syndrome. They describe, in detail, his irritability and rage. They often tell me that he's been verbally or physically abusive. Most go on to say that they love their husband and want to do everything they can to help him so that they can return to the good relationship they remember having before he got IMS.

I shudder when I get these kinds of letters. I have no quarrel with each woman's desire to help her man and to rescue their relationship, but I do have concerns about her priorities and the focus of her attention. Too many of these women remain in abusive, sometimes violent relationships, focusing their attention on helping *him* before thinking about helping *themselves*. I imagine myself reaching through the airwaves and shaking them. "Don't you know that you can't help him or help the relationship until you first help yourself?" I also fantasize shaking the men. "Don't you know how destructive your behavior is to your wife, your family, yourself?"

IRRITABLE MALES BECOME ADDICTED TO RAGE

When we talk about addiction, most people think about drugs like heroin or cocaine. Addicts are seen as people who have little self-respect and can't control their behavior. But having worked with addictions for more than 40 years, I have a broader view. I believe that people can become addicted to anything that can bring feelings of well-being, however short-lived, or can provide relief from pain, no matter how temporary.

With this understanding we can see how some people become addicted to gambling, pornography, the Internet, other people, or strong emotions. All of these behaviors can give people feelings of pleasure or well-being or can provide relief from pain or unhappiness.

Let's first take a look at how men can become hooked on rage. Most people confuse rage with anger. John Lee, author of *The Anger Solution*, says, "Rage is as different from anger as night is from day, as apples are from orangutans. Anger is a feeling and emotion. Rage has the ability to cover other feelings, but it is not a feeling or emotion in itself. Rage is like a huge dose of morphine. It is a drug that is legal, plentiful, readily available, and can be addictive."

The reason why rage can become addictive is that it doesn't satisfy a real need. Anger, on the other hand, is an emotion that expresses our need to defend ourselves against the loss of something we value. Rage is a cover for past losses and so can continue to escalate without end. Rage can be loud and aggressive or it can be quiet and passive. Rage can be expressed with slaps and punches or with mean looks and cutting words. Have you noticed that as rage is expressed, it tends to feed upon itself?

Lee offers a number of helpful contrasts between anger and rage:

- Anger clears the air, while rage clouds communication.
- Anger rights injustices and wrongs. Rage is an injustice and wrongs people further.
- Anger concerns the present. Rage concerns the past.
- Anger is about "me," about how I'm feeling. Rage is about "you," my judgment of your perceived inadequacies.

Men who get hooked on rage are looking for love, but don't know how to find it. They hunger for someone to love and comfort them, but they settle for trying to control those they have become dependent upon. They feel powerless and small and their rage gives them a temporary feeling of strength and superiority.

THE WOMEN WHO LOVE IMS MEN BECOME ADDICTED TO THEM

In his book *Love and Addiction,* Stanton Peele described the connection between "love" and "addiction" this way: "Many of us are addicts, but we don't know it. We turn to each other out of the same needs that drive some people to drink and others to heroin. Interpersonal addiction—love addiction—is just about the most common, yet least recognized, form of addiction we know."

Many women are taught from childhood to put other people's needs above their own. They are raised to be caregivers. As children they often take care of their parents, siblings, or friends. Such women may grow up with many unmet needs, choosing mates who seem secure and caring on the surface, but who are actually quite wounded. These wounded men often suffer from IMS as adults. And these wounded women are often the ones who fall in love with them.

In my book, *Looking for Love in All the Wrong Places: Overcoming Romantic and Sexual Addictions,* I describe the experiences that many women have with relationships. "Many of us are unhappy with our romantic relationships, but don't know what to do about it. There are times we swear 'never again.' Getting close is just too painful. But there is only so much energy we can devote to our jobs, our friends, our hobbies. Sooner or later we return to the search for love. When we finally find that special someone, we cling to them like orphaned children. Even when the relationship goes bad, we hold on for dear life. We can't seem to let go, even when the relationship is harming us. We ride a roller coaster of hope and despair." Does this sound at all familiar to you?

WHAT DO YOU NEED TO DO?

1. Understand that this journey is first and foremost about you.

Even though I call this problem "irritable male syndrome," it is not just a problem that men have. If IMS has come into your life, it is an opportunity for you to engage in your own healing. Although my own irritability and anger had been causing problems in our relationship for years, it wasn't until Carlin began to work on her own issues that things started to change.

For many women, focusing on themselves seems selfish. But, in fact, it's the only thing that can make things better for you, for him, and for the relationship. I would ask you to write out this phrase or put the sentiment into your own words and place it where you can read it every day. "I am committed to my own health and well-being. In order to help my man and help the relationship, I must first help myself. I'm loveable and capable and I deserve to have a joyful life."

2. Make a commitment to your own physical and emotional safety.

If you are being physically abused, that must stop. You must treat yourself like you would a precious child who is in danger. You must do whatever it takes to keep yourself from harm. If you have to move out of the house, you need to do that. If he has to move out of the house, you need to insist on it. Whatever it takes, you must create a safe place for yourself.

This must include emotional safety, as well as physical safety. Some us believe that if we aren't being physically abused then we are not being abused. But anyone who has been the recipient of rage, whether the rage is expressed with overt anger or covert contempt, knows how destructive that can be. In many ways emotional abuse is even more damaging than physical abuse. You need to commit to getting yourself out of emotionally abusive situations.

You may not be able to accomplish this immediately, but you must be willing to make the commitment to bring this about. Nothing will improve until you feel safe. If you grew up in an abusive family where you were abused directly or witnessed abuse, abuse will feel familiar. Feeling safe will feel foreign. In spite of whatever resistance you have, safety is where you must be.

3. Reach out for support.

When IMS comes into a relationship, many people find themselves withdrawing from friends and family. Consciously, or unconsciously, we feel ashamed. We don't want others to know about what's really going on with us. If the man is frightened and threatened he may not want you to talk to others. He may try to convince you that this is a private matter between you and him, and no one else should know about it.

You need to be willing to reach out in spite of your shame or his fear. Talk to a friend, tell a family member. Let them know that things are not okay at home and that you're committed to making things better. You don't have to violate confidences between him and you. But you do need to reach out to someone, friend, family member, or therapist. You can't heal by yourself.

4. Learn to understand your co-dependence.

Most people who are involved with an IMS male, and many who aren't, are co-dependent. The term was first used to describe people who were in a relationship with a drug addict or alcoholic. However, it really goes way beyond that. Charles Whitfield, author of *Co-Dependence: Healing the Human Condition*, says, "Co-dependence is a disease of lost selfhood. We become co-dependent when we turn our responsibility for our life and happiness over to our ego (our false self) and to other people. Co-dependents become so preoccupied with others that they neglect their True Self—who they really are." Does this sound at all like you? If so, make a commitment to reconnect with your true self. Many women can benefit from a women's support group or a 12 Step program such as Co-Dependents Anonymous.

5. Release your belief that you can fix your man.

Your man can get better. Your relationship can improve. But you can't fix him. In order for things to improve you have to accept that you are powerless to change him. You are powerless over his beliefs, his thoughts, his feelings, his decisions, and his behavior.

As you admit your powerlessness over his life, you will begin to recognize that you have total power over your life. You have total control over your beliefs, your thoughts, your feelings, your decisions, and your behavior. You won't feel your power immediately, but little by little you will find you are re-claiming your own selfhood. You will also recognize that your life will become richer, with him or without him. It's a great feeling.

What you'll also find is that as you change your own life for the better, his life will change for the better as well. Although you can't fix him, you can create the conditions that will help him to fix the problems that are causing his irritability and anger. Many women worry that if they can't fix their man, then there is no hope for their future. Many also feel guilty for focusing attention on themselves. But as you will find out, there are many ways to engage a man in a healing process and it starts with your willingness to heal yourself.

In this space, write down your thoughts. Are you willing to focus on "you" first and foremost?   Are you willing to make a commitment to your own safety and well-being? What does it feel like to save yourself first?

NOTES

NOTES

Chapter 3: What's Shame Got to Do With It? (Hint...Everything).

Dear Dr. Jed,

I have read your article and wonder if my husband suffers from any of this. We have been married for 19 years and I have just found out that 3 years ago he was unfaithful with the same woman we both knew. He is trying very hard right now to "make it up to me", but my heart is broken and I am a constant wreck. It is difficult for me to continue to support him; however I know I must find it in me. He does take comfort in my needing him, but still at times continues with the anger issues, drinking, sexual aggression, and paranoia.

I know he feels ashamed of the affair, but something more is going on. He seems to have a distorted view of reality. He doesn't understand why I love him so much. He doesn't understand why I want him around at all. He has considered suicide but I think I have gotten him away from that.

My husband and I have always known he was abused as a child, but he has no memory of anything before the age of 12, which is the year in which his grandfather took over with him and basically raised him from there. His parents are very abusive people that divorced when my husband was 20. They continue to try and "punish" people around them for everything. For the past 10 years or so, I have been thinking the increased anger, frustration, sexual aggression and self destructiveness may be an indication of sexual abuse instead of beatings. I wonder if he does remember sometimes, but is scared to tell anyone or has a fear of reliving it while telling the story. How do I let him know that no matter the type of abuse, my love for him is not a tap I can turn off, it's there forever whether he decides to stay with me or not. I will always love him. How do I get him to open up? Please help. CL.

What's shame have to do with *Irritable Male Syndrome?* Well, in a word, everything! It's like an invisible, yet poisonous, vapor that permeates relationships that are suffering from IMS. Although shame can have a profoundly negative impact on the lives of women, shame can be particularly devastating to guys. Although things like hormonal fluctuations, biochemical changes in the brain, stress, and loss of male identity are key causes of IMS; shame is the emotion that fuels IMS and keeps its destructive power alive in your relationship. Understanding how to deal with your man's shame will go a long way towards helping you both heal from the effects of IMS.

"Shame," says author Merle Fossum, "is feeling alone in the pit of unworthiness. Shame is not just a low reading on the thermometer of self-esteem. Shame is something like cancer—it grows on its own momentum." Both shame and guilt are ways in which people experience feeling bad. Yet the two are quite different. *Guilt* involves feeling bad about what we do or fail to do. *Shame* is feeling bad about who we are, about our very being. The shame that men experience is a kind of soul murder, undermining the foundations of our masculine selves. Women, too, feel the effects of shame. It's the kind of poison that can destroy lives.

SHAME AND VIOLENCE

Whether we are dealing with irritability, anger, or outright aggression, IMS is about violence. In understanding a problem, it is often helpful to see how it manifests in its most extreme forms so that we can better understand the less obvious ways it may affect our lives. To understand IMS in the average guy, it's helpful to explore the way shame leads to aggression in the most violent men. James Gilligan, M.D. has spent his professional career working in prisons with the most violent offenders. In his long career he has studied the underlying causes of violence and has come to a startling conclusion. In his book, *Violence,* he says, "I have yet to see a serious act of violence that was not provoked by the experience of feeling shamed and humiliated, disrespected and ridiculed, and that did not represent the attempt to prevent or undo this 'loss of face'—no matter how severe the punishment, even if it includes death."

The feeling of shame occurs inside us and can happen when we are alone, but it is most strongly felt before an audience, an external judge in whose eyes (and by comparison with whom) we appear weak, failed, foolish, incompetent, ridiculous, rejected, inferior, contemptible—in short shameful.

When Gilligan asked inmates why they had assaulted some-one, he heard the same answer over and over again. It was because he "disrespected me." The word "disrespect is so central in the vocabulary, moral value system, and psychodynamics of chronically violent men, Gilligan tells us, that they have abbrevi-ated it into the slang term, "he dis'ed me."

As one man told Gilligan, "I may be in prison, but I still have to have my pride, dignity, and self-esteem. And I'll kill every mother-fucker in that cell block if I have to in order to get it." Our prisons are full of men who would do anything, even kill or be killed, in order to avoid the shame they feel when they are disrespected.

Gilligan goes on to reveal a secret that is at the core of these men's lives. "The secret is that they feel ashamed—deeply ashamed, chronically ashamed, acutely ashamed, over matters that are so trivial that their very triviality makes it even more shameful to feel ashamed about them, so that they are ashamed even to reveal what shames them."

Having worked in prisons and having talked to many of the same kinds of men who Gilligan has talked with over the years, I know that we are not so different. I've carried the same secret that so many of them carry—the secret shame of feeling ashamed. I suspect that the man in your life also has that same secret. In order to help him and help yourself, you need to understand the shame that men bury deep inside—often hidden so deeply they are not even aware of it themselves.

By focusing on the shame men feel, I don't for a minute want to suggest that women don't carry a great deal of shame also. Every day women are subjected to a host of indignities and dis-counts. Here, I'm focusing on men since women often don't recognize the hidden shame men feel. Men are rarely aware of it and even less likely to talk about it when they are aware.

MEN'S SECRET SHAME

1. The shame of competition and rejection.

Males often remember, with a great deal of shame, walking across a room and asking the "cute" girl to dance, only to be turned down and having to walk back to his seat feeling that all eyes are on him and imagining people saying to themselves, "loser, loser, loser." This is the essence of male shame. We are always in competition with other males to be chosen by a female who can trigger our feelings of insufficiency and inadequacy with a casual shake of her head. And our shame deepens as others witness our retreat.

2. The shame of her "size" and "power."

Most women are not aware of the power they hold over men just by being female. Think about this. All of us are born from the body of a woman, but only men (in heterosexual relationships) have an intimate relationship with a person who is the same sex as the mother.

All men have a body memory of being small and totally dependent on a woman who is big, strong, and imposing. He may appear big and strong as an adult, but inside he still feels vulnerable. He never forgets that it was a woman who held his life in her hands, whose displeasure might cause her to abandon him to his death. This creates an inherent sense of shame that men feel when they are around women, but it's a shame that neither the man nor the woman is conscious of him having.

3. The shame of wanting to return to the comfort of infancy.

There's a joke that men spend nine months trying to get out and the rest of their lives trying to get back in. It's often used to illustrate men's preoccupation with sex, but it may hold a deeper truth. Women trigger men's desire to return to the safety, comfort, and warmth he remembered as a child—even back to the memory of being in the womb. I remember many times in my life feeling crushed by my battles in the world and wanting nothing more than to return to the comfort and warmth of childhood. But the thought was so frightening and shameful, I immediately blocked in out.

If I could have allowed the thought to surface it might have been something like this: "It's so damn hard being a man in the world, always competing, always fighting my way to the top, always struggling to make a living and supporting a family. I just want to rest. I want to crawl into my wife's arms and let her hold me. But if I ever let myself do that I know I'd never want to leave. I'd forfeit my manhood, she would hate me, cast me out, and that would be the end of me. I've got to erase that thought and never let it return."

This shameful longing seems to be universal. As anthropologist David Gilmore writes in his book, *Misogyny: The Male Malady,* men throughout the world have "unconscious wishes to return to infancy, longings to suckle at the breast, to return to the womb, the powerful temptation to surrender one's masculine autonomy to the omnipotent mother of childhood fantasy."

4. The shame of men's dependency on women.

In his book *Fire in the Belly: On Being a Man*, psychologist Sam Keen talks about his hidden dependency on women. "If the text of my life was 'successful, independent man,' the subtext was 'engulfed by WOMAN." Keen goes on to describe the ways in which the archetypal WOMAN (and hence all real-life women to a significant degree) rules our lives. "The secret men seldom tell, and often do not know (consciously) is the extent to which our lives circle around our relationships to WOMAN...She is the audience before whom the dramas of our lives are played out. She is the judge who pronounces us guilty or innocent. She is the Garden of Eden from which we are exiled and the paradise for which our bodies long. She is the goddess who can grant us salvation and the frigid mother who denies us."

It's no wonder there are times that we "hate" the woman we feel so dependent upon. We long to let ourselves melt into her arms, but our shame causes us to deny our need and project our anger on to her. If we can't accept our own needs to be nurtured and cared for, we will have a difficult time feeling love for the woman in our lives.

5. The shame of women's words.

Often women assume that men are "tough" and your words won't hurt him. In part this is a result of our inaccurate gender assumptions. Many believe that women are more delicate and easily hurt, and men are stronger and can take more punishment. The truth is that men are very vulnerable to women's words. He is likely to cover his pain because he feels ashamed to admit that what she said may have cut him to the core.

Patricia Love and Steven Stosny remind us that "Words hurt. Words destroy. Words can kill a relationship." In their book, *How to Improve Your Marriage Without Talking About It,* they detail some of the most common things that women say that trigger shame in a man, including:

- Correcting what he says, "It was last Wednesday, not Thursday."
- Giving unsolicited advice: "If you would just make the call you'll feel better."
- Implying inadequacy: "I wish you had been at that workshop with me (not because he would have enjoyed it but because it would have "corrected some of his flaws").
- Focusing on what you didn't do, not what you did: "It would have been better if you'd said 'I'm sorry' to begin with."
- Using a harsh tone: "I'm so tired of this!"
- Condescending: "Someday maybe you'll learn to pick up after yourself."
- Making "you" statements: "You make me so mad I can't think straight."
- Expecting him to make me happy: "If we just did more fun things together..."

As with fear-triggers in men, women often aren't aware of the things they say that trigger shame in a man. Women are generally much more facile with words than men and are more used to verbal jousting. They often wound without meaning to because they aren't aware of the power of their words.

WHAT YOU CAN DO TO HELP REDUCE SHAME IN MEN

1. Put yourself in his shoes.

The most important thing you can do is to be aware of the "put-downs" that men have suffered and continue to suffer in their lives. Just putting yourself in his shoes and having compassion for his experience can go a long way towards healing. You don't have to figure out what to say. In fact, as I point out in Chapter 22, talking can often trigger shame in men. You just have to feel with him and accept that his irritability, anger, withdrawal are not meant to hurt you. They are often the best he can do at the moment to protect against shame.

2. Watch your words.

You can also notice the ways that you have contributed to his shame by things you may have inadvertently said. You need to watch that you don't shame yourself when you notice hurtful things you may have said to him. Just apologize sincerely when you do it and increase your awareness so you don't do it again. You also need to stop saying things to friends or family that are shaming towards your man. Sharing your negativity may offer temporary relief and make you feel closer to a girlfriend, but it will undermine your relationship with your man.

3. Help him accept being touched and nurtured.

We all long to be held, touched, and nurtured. Yet men, even more than women, are touch deprived. This begins in childhood because boys are touched less, and less lovingly than girls. As we grow up, we often associate being "manly" with being tough, independent, and self-sufficient.

Nothing could be further from the truth. We all need to be held and nurtured from the day we are born until the day we die. As Dr. Sue Johnson says in her excellent book, *Hold Me Tight: Seven Conversations for a Lifetime of Love,* "Contact with a loving partner literally acts as a buffer against shock, stress, and pain." Help him learn to touch and be touched. It will go a long way to reducing his shame and creating a closer bond between you.

In chapter 22 you will learn more about the way your fear and his shame interact and what you can do to reduce his shame by reducing your fear.

Here's your chance to write down some things about shame. How have you been shamed in your own life? What aspects of shame may be affecting the man in your life? What things have you done that may have inadvertently contributed to increasing shame in him? Are you willing to do what you can to change things?

NOTES

NOTES

Chapter 4: What Are The Things I Can Do Right Away to Keep the Relationship From Going Under?

Dear Dr. Diamond,

Five years ago my husband turned 50. Since, then, our lives have been turned upside down. I feel I have been wandering in the wilderness trying to understand what is going on. We've had our ups and downs during the 24 years we have been married, but I've thought, on the whole, we've been happy.

Just when I thought we could really enjoy our time together my husband has totally changed. At first, little things bothered him. If I didn't have dinner prepared at the exact time I promised, he'd snap at me. When I got in a slight car accident, he nearly went ballistic and accused me of driving like a maniac.

When I ask him what's wrong, he either ignores me or screams at me. When I reach out to touch him, he pulls away like my touch is poison. He tells me, "I love you, but I'm not in love with you. I think I should leave." That cuts me to the bone. How can a man who recently told me he was more in love with me than when we got married all of a sudden decide that he is no longer in love? What can I do? I'm terrified that I'm losing my husband, my lover, my best friend. Please help us. DT.

One of the most difficult challenges for the women I work with is to deal with the sudden changes that the man goes through when IMS strikes. For most couples IMS hits them at mid-life. They have often passed through the stage of getting their careers going and raising their children. Now they feel they can relax and are looking forward to having some time for themselves.

She pictures a trip to Europe (or with the economy the way it is, at least some time at a near-by romantic get-away.) She's worked hard to make their marriage work and now she's looking forward to enjoying the fruits of her labors. Then, out of the blue, she hears these dreaded words, "I love you, but I'm not *in love* with you anymore. I think I should leave." As DT says, the words cut to the bone and leave women feeling wounded, desperate, and terrified.

Although repairing the damage caused by IMS can take some time, there are things a woman can do right away to keep the relationship from going under, including the following:

1. Take a deep breath. Don't panic.

When IMS first strikes, it feels like you've been punched in the gut. You literally have the breath knocked out of you. You feel immobilized, numb, and don't know what to do; but you feel you must do something immediately or your life will surely fall apart. Take a deep breath. Don't panic. You are probably in shock and your body, mind, and spirit, are on red alert. Breathe again. Try to relax. Go talk to a friend or trusted family member. Let someone hold you until you have regained a sense of balance and calm. (If there's no one around, wrap your arms around yourself.)

You may have to return to step 1 multiple times over the next few weeks and months. Don't worry. That's part of the process. When you're ready, move on to step 2.

2. Reach out and connect with what is stable in your life.

When IMS strikes it feels like your whole life is turned upside down. But it really hasn't! The man in your life is going through a major change and it is affecting you in important and profound ways, but that is not your whole world. Ask yourself what is stable in your life—work, children, friends, your home, your health, your favorite clothes, a favorite place? When you're in crisis mode, you first need to "ground" yourself. You do that by connecting with the people and things that you can count on.

3. Just say "no"!

What did you do when your teenager said, "I don't love you anymore and I'm going to move out?" If you didn't go through this stage, you can imagine it. You took a deep breath and said to yourself, "Yes, he might run away and that wouldn't be good. But chances are this is a stage he's going through and things will work out." Mid-life is not the same as puberty, but it has some things in common. There's lots of drama, a lot of emotional ups and downs. When you understand what's going on, you can keep your cool.

If the man in your life talks about leaving, say to yourself, "No, that's not what I want. I will do what I can to understand what is going on and work things out." Sometimes you can say the words out loud. "I know you're unhappy and we'll have to make some changes to make things right, but leaving is not the answer. I don't want you to do that." And you can take another deep breath, walk out of the room, and get on with your day.

4. Remember his brain is locked on to the "old witch," but it can change back to the "young woman."

Women often make comments like the one by DT at the beginning of the chapter. They wonder how the man can change from looking at her with love and affection to giving her looks filled with hate and revulsion. One visual aid that helps them to understand what is going on is to recall the optical illusion of the "old-witch/young woman."

What do you see? Is it a profile of a young and beautiful lady, or do you see an old witch with huge and ugly nose?

You can't see them both at the same time. Our brain organizes what it sees as one or the other. (If you're having trouble seeing one or the other, the part which is the old woman's nose is the young woman's jaw. Her head is turned away from you. The old woman's left eye is the girl's ear, and the old woman's mouth is the young one's necklace. The tiny lump that looks like the old woman's wart on her nose is the nose of the young woman.)

When a man's brain gets locked on to the "witch," he sees you as ugly and dangerous. He is sure you want to harm him (or in his deepest fears, eat him alive). With that view of you, it's no wonder he acts the way he does. It helps to remember that you haven't changed. He's got brain lock. But never fear, his brain can unlock and see the beauty again. He just needs the right guidance to bring that about.

In the meantime, keep your brain focused on viewing yourself as the beauty. It is very easy to begin to believe his negative view of you. Though it may be difficult, you need to remind yourself over and over again that you are beautiful and wonderful and things will work out, with him or without him.

5. Stand up for yourself.

When you're afraid he's going to leave, and you believe if he does your life will come to an end, you will try to do anything to keep him close. This can include accepting his judgments, blame, and bad temper. Don't do that. It doesn't help him. It doesn't help you. And it doesn't protect your relationship.

As scary as it is, you must stand up for yourself and tell him you care about him, but you won't let yourself be abused. You need to say something like this: "I know how angry and frustrated you are. At times you feel there is no hope for our relationship and that I am the cause of all your problems. God knows I have my faults, but this isn't all about me. Your anger and blame are not helping things. I love you and care about you, but you have to stop taking it out on me. Let's work together to figure out what's wrong."

You will put this in your own words and repeat them over and over in different ways. But there are three messages you want to convey to him:

1. I know you are angry, frustrated, worried, etc. (to pinpoint his feelings, see which ones predominate when you take the quiz in chapter 18 and look at the different types of IMS later in the book) and you have a right to feel that way. I feel that way too.

2. We need to work together to make things better for both of us.

3. In the mean time, I won't allow any abuse.

"I was afraid that standing up to him would enrage him even more," a 44-year-old client confided, "but I was totally surprised when the reverse occurred. He actually calmed down a bit and began to talk about his feelings."

In this space, write down your thoughts. What things have you tried that you hoped would make things better? What worked? What didn't work? Which of the five practices listed above are you willing to try? It may take time to see positive results, but keep trying. Different approaches work for different people and some approaches need to be tried over and over before they catch on.

NOTES

Chapter 5: What Should I Do When He Says, "I Love You, But I'm Not *In Love* With You Anymore"?

Dear Jed,

*My husband and I have been married for 28 years now and we have been very close to each other for nearly all that time. But he recently told me, "I love you, but I'm not **in love** with you." I felt like I'd been kicked. We've always had a very passionate and intimate relationship and this came out of the blue.*

Since then, he's become even more withdrawn and mean towards me. I don't understand this dramatic change in him. He's very distant with me and doesn't even want me to touch him, as if I have germs. It's so frustrating. I sometimes think that he's fooling around, but he says he's not, and I guess I believe him. I want to ask him questions to get to the bottom of things, but he's always so angry I'm afraid to approach him. I love him and can't see this happening to us. Please let me know what I should do to save this marriage and our relationship. Please help me! EP.

For most of us, the dreaded words, "I love you, but I'm not *in love* with you," are devastating. They chill us to the bone, as we fear for our relationship. They bring back memories from the past when we loved someone deeply, but they just wanted to be "friends." They force us to recall intimate relationships that came to an end with the other person being "nice" and trying to let us down easy. For us it felt like we were being stabbed in the heart with a knife. Remember?

If this is happening to you, there are things you can do.

1. Understand the added weight that past losses impose.

You need to recognize that the present experience has added weight because of the losses we have experienced in the past. Although we've all had relationships that ended hurtfully and most of us have put them behind us, they can still be triggered, full force, when we feel that an important relationship is threatened.

2. Get support.

Many of us had close friends in the past with whom we'd share every little detail of our lives, our triumphs and our disappointments. Some of us have lost those close relationships; others of us feel a little ashamed of sharing these kinds of adult pains with our friends. "I didn't want to admit to anyone that my husband was pulling away from me," a 44-year-old mother of three told me. "I felt ashamed that his actions were so devastating to me. I'm not an insecure teen-ager after all."

The fear that we may be losing someone we love can be as overwhelming when we're fifty as when we're fifteen. Don't try and deal with this on your own. Reach out and share it with someone you trust.

3. Understand the "falling in love" feeling.

Let's take another look at that feeling we call "falling in love." Perhaps the best description of being *in love* is in the book *Love and Limerence: The Experience of Being in Love* by social scientist Dr. Dorothy Tennov. She begins her book with a description we can all identity with:

"You think: I want you. I want you forever, now, yesterday, and always. Above all, I want you to want me. No matter where I am or what I am doing, I am not safe from your spell. At any moment, the image of your face smiling at me, of your voice telling me you care, or of your hand in mine, may suddenly fill my consciousness rudely pushing out all else. The expression 'thinking of you' fails to convey either the quality or quantity of this unwilled mental activity. 'Obsessed' comes closer but leaves out the aching."

The connection to "obsession" or "addiction" is a good one. When we are "in love" our brains are bathed in neurochemicals that are similar to cocaine. It's no wonder the feeling is so strong or that we want to hold on to it as long as we can. But most of us recognize that we can't stay "in love" forever. We remember the early years of a relationship with a deep longing, but don't try to hold on to that feeling.

There's a good biological reason for us to be possessed by limerence (intense romantic desire) in the first two or three years of a relationship. Being obsessed with our partner is the best way to keep us locked together long enough to make a couple of children to keep the human race going. That's why this "in love" feeling is so intense and powerful. After the obsession of "being in love" wears off, it is replaced by a deeper, more satisfying love that includes such things as friendship, respect, understanding, commitment, care, and comfort.

4. Change the way you think about love.

When we use the same word "love" to mean both the initial obsession and the later mature stage of love, we set ourselves up for pain. For most women, being "in love" and "loving you" merge together. They can feel just as much "in love" after twenty-eight years as they were in the first few years. Many men experience the "in love" phase and the "love you" phase as separate. If you can say to yourself he's telling me, "I love you, but I'm no longer in limerence with you," it won't feel quite so painful.

He's not telling you he doesn't love you, but that the limerence has worn off. You might be temped to say something like, "Of course it's worn off. What did you expect after 28 years? Love changes, it grows deeper. It may not be as crazy and hot, but it is more nourishing and satisfying. Don't you understand that?"

You might also be tempted to remind him of the words of Playwright George Bernard Shaw who gave us this humorous commentary on the traditional marriage ceremony. "When two people are under the influence of the most violent, most insane, most delusive, and most transient of passions, they are required to swear that they will remain in that excited, abnormal, and exhausting condition continuously until death do them part."

But the man is telling you something more than "I've fallen out of limerence with you." He's saying he misses that crazy-totally-entranced-obsessed-head-over-heels "in love" feeling that he once had. We can all appreciate the sentiment. In the same way that many of us miss the rush we remember when we first got high on drugs, many people long for the rush they remember when they first fell in love.

So, what do you do? Here are some things I have found will work.

1. Move beyond your fear to hear what he needs and what you need.

When we're afraid, all we can think about are the disasters we're sure lie ahead. We ruminate over increasingly dramatic and tragic occurrences: "He's not in love with me anymore. He doesn't think I'm attractive. He's probably going to leave me. If he leaves me, I couldn't handle it. No one would ever want me. I'm a total failure as a spouse. I'm going to be all alone the rest of my life." Does any of this sound familiar?

Get a hold of yourself. Don't go down that path. Ask yourself, "What is he needing"? He may be telling you he needs to recapture his passion for life. A man may say he is no longer "in love" with his wife," but what is really going on is that he is no longer "in love" with his life. Talk to him about where he feels stuck and what things might excite him. Tune in to your own needs and talk about what things excite you. It may take time, but with patience he will open up to you and reveal that he's lost some of his life passion. You may have lost some as well. Together you can recapture what was lost and find new forms of passion.

2. Become the new woman of his dreams.

When you think about it, men's biology has a tendency to push them towards other women. All women reach a point, usually by age 50, when they can no longer reproduce. Men are able to have children later in life. For women, there's no reproductive advantage to leaving her partner to find someone younger and more attractive. For men, that isn't the case.

He may love his spouse and want to be with her forever, but there is a biological pull, usually unconscious, that says, "Look, staying with a woman who can't have more children isn't going to get more of your genes into the next generation. Better to fall out of love with her and fall in love with someone who can still make babies."

Rather than ignore this biological reality, you can make it work for you. You don't have to go on a diet and get back to the weight you were when you were 20 or get your body plucked, peeled, and perked to look like a 25-year-old. But you can take care of yourself, feel and look good at whatever age you are. You can make changes in your attitude and appearance to become a new you.

There's a story. Maybe it's even true. A woman puts her profile up on a dating site. She focuses on the good qualities she has and thinks about the kind of man she'd like to meet. An interesting stranger answers her ad and the way he describes himself seems exciting and dreamy. And yes, it turns out it's her husband.

You don't have to go that far. You can break up the old mind-set that says, "we're an old married couple" and think like the girl you were when you were excited about finding that special someone. It can be fun to reinvent ourselves periodically.

Of course, you have to confront his possible infidelity. You can reinvent yourself, but if he is "out looking" and "falls in love," it's very difficult to get him focused on you. So don't wait until things get bad before you commit to a "new relationship."

My wife, Carlin, and I have been married more than 30 years. After we had been married for 15 years, we decided to "start over," to create a new focus for our lives together. We went away and had a re-marriage ceremony and a re-honeymoon. What could you do to become the new woman of his dreams? Of course, it can be scary and also exciting for both of you to re-invent yourselves for each other.

3. You can't keep your relationship alive unless you're willing to lose it.

Most all of us are afraid of losing the one we love. It's so frightening that we do everything we can to block the fear out of our minds. When something happens like him saying, "I'm not *in love* with you," many women do everything they can to hold the relationship together.

But think about those early days of passion and promise. One of the things that made it so exciting was that we didn't know for sure that the relationship would last. Remember how we'd agonize over something our partner said that we thought might indicate they didn't really love us. And remember the feeling of ecstatic joy when they touched us and gave us that special look that made us know "yes, we are loved."

At the beginning of a relationship we don't have as much to lose. We can afford to take some risks and try new things, reveal parts of ourselves we're not sure will be accepted. Living on the edge of possibility is part of what keeps the relationship exciting. If we remember that, we can take the risk to speak our truth even when we're afraid it might endanger the relationship.

In any long-term relationship there are important thoughts and feelings, desires and dreams that get suppressed because we're afraid that revealing them would not be accepted. For many of us, the passion and excitement we thought we had lost can be re-kindled by taking risks to tell each other the truth about who we are, what we're feeling, and what we need.

In this place you can write down your thoughts and feelings. What scares you the most in your relationship? What can you do to develop the courage to move towards your fears? What are you willing to do to create a new relationship with the guy you are with?

NOTES

Chapter 6: How Should I React When He Says He Needs "Time for Himself" But I'm Afraid He's About to Leave?

Dear Dr. Jed,

I just received your newsletter. It really sounds like my husband may have IMS. Three months ago he told me he hasn't been happy for 2 or 3 years. He said he can be happy at work, but when he comes home he's unhappy and just doesn't want to be here. He has been extremely irritable, short-tempered, and mean for the last couple of years. He had open heart surgery 2 years ago. I feel that that is when his personality changed.

He says he loves me, that I'm attractive, a good wife and mother, but says he needs time to find himself. He says I'm not the problem, there's something wrong with him. He tells me that there's something missing, and that "life is too short to be unhappy."

I want to help him, but I don't want to lose him. I give him as much time alone as he wants, but it doesn't seem to help. He stays at home as little as possible but when he's home he is angry most of the time. I feel I'm always walking on egg shells trying to keep him from exploding. When I ask him what he needs, he gets very angry and sometimes cries and says he doesn't have any answers for me. Any advice or suggestions? ML.

I've counseled more than 25,000 men and women over the last 44 years. I would say that most of the people I see have some fear of abandonment. Most of us grew up in homes where one or both parents were absent or where relationships were chaotic or distant. We long for the security of love because it nourishes our adult soul, but also because we are trying to fill an inner void that opened up in childhood.

Whenever we feel that someone we love and depend upon may leave, it brings up a great deal of confusion and fear. Even if the relationship has been stressful, even when we may feel we'd be better off without that angry person in our lives, we still fear being alone. The first thing to do is to acknowledge our fear of abandonment and understand a bit more about how it fits in with our lives.

Remember, regardless of how old we are now or how successful we have been in our lives, we were all helpless infants at one time and our physical and emotional survival depended on having a parent who would attend to our needs 24 hours a day. From the first moments of conception the mother was our primary caregiver—the person who fed us, sheltered us, protected us, comforted us, held us in her arms to allay our fears. It is with our mothers that we make our first attachment, with her who we form the bonds that determine our survival and sense of security.

If we are lucky, there are also fathers who sing to us, play with us, throw us in the air, and keep us close and safe. But it is the woman who holds the primary position in our inner life, a woman who is the object of our most profound attachment, a woman who becomes our first love object. As we'll see, this has profound implications on the way men and women deal with their fears of abandonment.

At one time we all were merged with the mother. Our blood stream and hers was intermixed. Whatever she felt, we felt. Whatever she put into her body went into our bodies. Yet we all had to separate from our primary attachment to our mother in order to become fully human. Thus separation and unity—being attracted to others and being attached to one person, seeking and merging— are themes that are central to our whole lives.

This process of separation, however, is different for females than it is for males. Since females will grow up to be the same sex as their mothers (I know that may seem obvious, but sometimes the most obvious things have the most profound implications), they don't have to try so hard to be "independent" and they keep a more primal sense of connection to their primary love object.

In order for males to grow up to be men, they have to try harder to differentiate themselves. They have to reject more of what is feminine in them in order to be different, a male, not a female. If they have a secure bond with a nurturing father this process is made easier.

Women, generally, feel more secure about themselves as women, than men feel about themselves as men. I know that may not be obvious, but from my experience it is true. Therefore in love relationships, women tend to find it easier to make a deep *connection.* This connection becomes the source of their security, even the cornerstone of their identity. Their greatest fear is of *abandonment* or *loss.*

When men fall in love, they find it more difficult to connect. Part of the reason is that they are secretly afraid that if they get too close they will merge back with the woman, lose their identity, and cease to exist. Few men are aware of this, and those who are, guard this secret with their lives. In fact, I may be in big trouble telling this to you now.

As a result men are conditioned to need *separation* and *space.* Their greatest fear is that they will lose their freedom, become *bound* or *trapped.*

So, now that you know some of the secrets, here's what you can do to save yourself and rescue your relationship.

1. Acknowledge your fear of abandonment and remind yourself you are no longer a child.

The more we try and suppress our fear and block it from consciousness the more our lives are ruled by childhood fears. We may be 40, 50, or 60 years old, but inside we feel that we are 4, 5, or 6 and our Mommy and Daddy are about to leave us and we will die. So, you need to remind yourself, over and over again, that you are an adult and you have adult fears, not childhood fears. You need to say to yourself, "I am worried that he may leave and I would be truly sad if that happened. But I'm an adult, not a child, and I have lots of supports in my life. It may be difficult, but I'm not going to die if he leaves."

2. Encourage him to take his space.

This is impossible to do if you're in your childhood emotional state. But when you get back to feeling like an adult you can recognize his need for space and encourage him to take it. You can tell him, "I know you need to feel free, that's very important to you, and you've been doing a great deal to take care of things at work and at home. I hear that you need time for yourself. What can I do to make that possible so you can take it without feeling guilty?"

Most men don't start out wanting to leave. They usually need space, time away to sort things out, to just think their own thoughts and feel their own feelings, but they don't feel their spouse would be supportive. Often their fears are unfounded, but they build up resentments believing they can't take time for themselves.

Sometimes they may take time away, but feel guilty afterwards. At other times they remain ever the dutiful husband, until one day they don't come home. Don't wait until that happens.

3. Put "leaving" on the table. Don't wait for him to do it.

I often work with people who are suicidal. One of the myths that many people still hold is that if you bring up the topic, it might be interpreted as encouraging the person to kill themselves. As a result, friends and family live in terror that the person they care about may take their own life. Yet, they avoid the topic at all costs.

The reality is that talking about suicide is a great relief for everyone involved. The same is true about "leaving." As soon as you talk about it, your own fear will diminish and so will the secrecy surrounding the issue. You might say something like this: "I hear that you need your own space and I'll do whatever I can to be supportive. But I also know that sometimes a person thinks that things would be better if they just left, rode off into the sunset, and started all over with a new life. Do you ever feel that way?"

He may tell you that he does. He may say he's not thinking of leaving, just wanting to have more time to himself. Either way, you're talking about what is most fearful to you, which is good. As you do that, the fear will dissipate and the intimacy between the two of you will increase.

4. Think about your own needs for freedom and space.

One of the things I've learned by counseling people all these years is that often one person in the couple is acting out the needs that the other person is afraid to acknowledge. Whether this is true for you or not in this instance, this is a good time to ask yourself about your own needs for freedom and space.

When was the last time you really took time for yourself? How long has it been since you took the kind of vacation that really nourished your soul? Play a little game with yourself. If you were to get into your car one day and just drive off into the sunset, what kind of life might you like to lead? Where would you go? What would you do? Who would you meet?

5. Set up some time with your spouse to talk about "time for..."

When I counsel men and women, I tell them that there are four kinds of "time for" needs that are important to their health and well-being. First, you need time for yourself. Next, you need time for yourselves as a couple. Third, you need time to be with members of your family. Fourth, you need time for friends and community.

For most families the "time fors" get out of balance. Sometimes you are working hard to support the family and not having time for yourself or for yourselves as a couple. At other times, you become lost in "togetherness" and are missing time alone. There's no magic formula. Each family has to work to find the proper balance. It will always be a work in progress. The important thing is to talk about it together.

This is a place to write down your thoughts and reactions. What are the things that particularly made sense to you in this chapter? What things will you do to gain a better sense of security, and to work with your fears of abandonment? How can you work out the balance of time together and time apart?

NOTES

NOTES

Chapter 7: If I Suspect There's Another Woman He's Gotten Involved With, What Should I Do?

Dear Dr. Jed,

My husband is forty-six years old and we have been married for twenty years. Shortly before our anniversary this past August, I noticed he seemed distant and somewhat irritable, and for him, almost nasty. Our marriage before this had been rather ordinary. I thought the reason for his mood changes was due to stress over finances, but I assumed things would be OK.

When I finally approached him about it, he simply said he didn't feel anything anymore and would really like to be on his own. He said he felt like he missed out on things when he was younger. He said he's not going through any kind of mid-life crisis, but he just wants to come and go as he pleases, which he has never done before.

Recently I discovered that he was developing a "relationship" with someone sixteen years younger than him. When we had a blowup over it, he said he broke it off completely. I don't understand what's going on and I don't know what I can trust. BL.

We've all heard the stories about the mid-life man who trades in his wife for another (usually younger) woman. It may be someone he works with, a "friend" who's become more than a friend, an old girl-friend, even an ex-wife. If it hasn't happened to you, it probably has to someone you know well. Am I right? You don't like to think about the possibility that it could happen in your family, but now you have your suspicions. What do you do? There are three possibilities most people consider and they're not necessarily mutually exclusive. At some point you may try each of the three and you may do so more than once: 1) you can ignore your fears and hope for the best, 2) ask him directly if he's involved with someone, or 3) become a "detective" and look for proof of his infidelity. Let's examine each in turn.

1. Ignore your fears and hope for the best.

Whatever the nature of our marriage vows, most of us agreed to be faithful to our partner. We wouldn't be together if we didn't have a deep trust for our partner, so confronting the possibility that he may be seeing someone else undermines our sense of security and our very sense of reality. Many women I talk to say *they* feel disloyal to question his honesty, even when they have ample reason to doubt him.

If it's someone else's relationship it may be easier to tell someone to confront the man and have it out. But when it's our relationship that is on the line, it isn't so easy to do.

2. Ask him directly if he's involved with someone.

Asking him directly might seem the most straightforward thing to do, but it has its own problems. What if he lies to you? How do you know if he's telling you the truth or covering himself? What if he tells you that you are being crazy to even think such a thing? What if it makes him even angrier than he's been and he becomes even meaner to you? You want to believe him, but you don't want to be made a fool of if he's not telling the truth. If you've been through this you know what I'm talking about. If you haven't, I'm sure you've thought about these kinds of questions.

3. Become a "detective" (or hire one) and look for proof of his infidelity.

No one wants to become suspicious of their partner and no one wants to change from a loving spouse into a detective. But sometimes not knowing is driving you crazy. You feel if you just knew the truth you could figure out what to do. You may begin checking his phone records or his credit card statements. You may listen in on phone calls. You feel sleazy having to do it. But you feel worse thinking about what may be going on behind your back. You'd rather know the truth than wonder what he's doing.

Stop right now. Whatever you've done or are thinking of doing, there's a better way. You still may want to do one or more of the actions listed above. But here's what I want you to do first:

1. Take a hard look at yourself and your relationship.

We get married for many reasons, most of them unconscious. Here are a few I've heard in therapy:

- "It was just the right time for me to settle down, I liked him, and he seemed to want me."
- "I had to get away from home and he was there for me."
- "I didn't want to be lonely and I was afraid I wouldn't find anyone else."
- "I was pregnant and thought I had to get married."
- "He liked me and he seemed to like my kids. They needed a father."
- "He was sexy and attractive and all my friends admired him."

Whatever mixture of reasons brought you together, you have to honestly answer these four questions if you're going to move ahead: 1. What are the benefits to you if you remain together? 2. What drawbacks would you face if you left? 3. What are the benefits you might receive if you left the marriage? What are the drawbacks if you stay?

Not easy questions, I know. You may have to spend a good deal of time answering them, but it will be worth it. You might think of the answers to questions 1 and 2 as weighing on one side of a balance scale and the answers to questions 3 and 4 on the other side. When you place staying or leaving on the balance, which one has the more weight?

2. Be honest about "deal breakers."

There are no simple answers to deciding whether to stay or leave, but you need to be honest about any possible deal breakers. For instance, if you find out that he's been seeing a girl from work after hours for a drink, is that a deal breaker, and would you leave the relationship, no matter what, if that were true? How about if he had been having a four-month affair with your best friend?

Remember, this is your relationship, not that of your friends, parents, or children. What someone else might consider a deal breaker, might not be so for you. What someone else could live with, maybe you could not.

3. Weigh the pros and cons of the relationship and decide if you want to stay and under what circumstances you would leave.

Many women tell me they want to know the truth, but when I suggest some possible truthful scenarios, they blanch, and it's clear they hadn't considered what knowing the truth might mean. In spite of some marriage vows where we pledge to stay "till death do we part," for most people there is a point at which we must leave a destructive relationship.

4. If you decide to stay, set a check-in date to re-evaluate your decision.

I've talked with clients who stayed too long in a destructive relationship and others who left too soon. Having a check-in date will help eliminate both possibilities. Remember you wouldn't be in this situation if there weren't some problems in the relationship. It will take some time to fix what can be fixed. Everyone has to set their own date for a check-in, but most people I work with make it a minimum of 90 days and a maximum of a year.

Having a time to re-evaluate gives you some boundaries to work with. Other than a "deal breaker" which would immediately end things, you know you have some time to work on the relationship. You also know that you won't just go on blindly, hoping against hope that things will improve.

5. Most people in this situation are having relationship problems. Find out what yours are.

I rarely hear from women or men who both tell me their relationship is wonderful. Their lives are great. They are madly in love. And they are having an affair with their next-door neighbor. I'll admit that many men and women have a tendency to put on a "happy face" and pretend everything is wonderful, even when it isn't. Even if it appears to you that his behavior has come out of the blue and you've both been totally happy, let's assume for now that there are some problems.

Again, take a fearless inventory. Ask yourself the following questions: What are the things in the relationship that you're unhappy about? What things might he be unhappy about that he hasn't talked about openly? What stresses have been going on in the rest of your lives that might be impacting the relationship?

6. Understand that some men (and women) can become attracted to others even when their relationship is fine.

Contrary to religious doctrine, fairy-tales, and the Ozzy and Harriet sit-coms many of us grew up with, we are all sexual and romantic beings who don't lose interest in others just because we enter a committed relationship. I'm not suggesting that its right (or wrong) or that you should accept his involvement if its taking place (that's why we talked about "deal breakers" earlier) I'm just saying the fact that someone may be interested, getting involved, or already involved with someone, doesn't necessarily mean there are problems in the relationship. Either way you'll need to address the question, as you'll see shortly.

7. Its time for a walk and talk.

The words a man dreads most hearing is "honey, we have to talk." So don't say them. There's a better way. Face-to-face communication frightens most men. It could be a genetic holdover from the time we were hunters when face-to-face communication occurred just before the wild animal ripped his throat out.

Far better to discuss important matters "side-by-side," a mode much more comfortable to men, and which occurs naturally when you walk and talk together. Remember that whatever comes up in the talk is within the context of making your lives more joyful. You may eventually ask him directly about whether he is seeing someone, but first you need to re-establish a caring connection.

Walking together, particularly if it's in a naturally beautiful setting, can be healing to your body, mind, and spirit and put you both in a mood for sharing your deepest feelings and needs.

8. You may benefit from a marriage counselor, but be sure it isn't a divorce counselor.

During the 44 years I've been in counseling, things have changed. Early on most counselors believed that all marriages could be fixed, and worked towards that end. Now, therapists focus more on individual happiness, and inadvertently (or directly) encourage the break up of marriages. If you're clear on your boundaries and you want the marriage to work out, pick a therapist who is as committed as you are.

This is your space to write down your thoughts. When your relationship is threatened it's difficult to think clearly. Write down the answers to the questions asked above. Look them over and let them guide your future.

NOTES

Chapter 8: What Should I Do if He Leaves or Threatens to Leave?

Dear Dr. Jed,

I was in my doctor's waiting room and just so happened to read an article in the grapevine magazine about "The Irritable Male Syndrome." This described my husband to a T. He's started to take things out on my children, getting very angry at them and bringing their confidence down. He would also degrade me about my weight and appearance and would call me names. He said that everything was my fault. I finally decided to take my kids away for a week to get away from him. We had a great time and I began to find myself again.

When I got back, I felt a lot better about myself and I had more faith that we could work out our problems. It seemed things were going better for a while, but his dark moods returned and one day he just announced that he was leaving. He got himself an apartment not far from here and he still comes around to see the kids, but he bristles when I try and talk to him about us. He doesn't seem happy. How do I get him to see what he is doing? It seems so obvious to me and everybody else, but he is just not willing to listen and still thinks I am the problem.

What makes it even harder is that I still love him and I think he loves me. I pray and hope we can get through this for each other and our children but I don't know what to do. If I wait until he comes to me he may never return. Every time I reach out to him he tells me I'm the problem. I wonder if I just have to move on with my life. Maybe my husband has to figure things out for himself. But it doesn't seem fair that my children and I have to go through this pain. I just don't know what to do. You are my last hope. Can you help me, my husband and our family? JP.

Many people spend a good part of their lives worrying about whether a spouse might leave. Some of you, I know, must actually deal with the consequences of a man's moving out. Although there are endless discussions and many books written about why men leave, few people get at the heart of the matter. In order for you to make the right decision you need to understand the secret reasons (which even most men never come to learn) about why they leave.

1. Men are more insecure than women.

Although men often act as though they are independent and self sufficient, they are inherently more insecure than women. Consider these facts about male vulnerability:

- More male than female embryos are conceived, possibly because the spermatozoa carrying the Y chromosome swim faster than those carry the X.
- External maternal stress around the time of conception is associated with a reduction in the male-to-female sex ratio, suggesting that the male embryo is more vulnerable than the female.
- The male fetus is at greatest risk of death or damage from almost all the obstetric catastrophes that can happen before birth. Perinatal brain damage, cerebral palsy, congenital deformities of the genitalia and limbs, premature birth, and stillbirth are all more common in boys.
- Boy's brains are slower to develop. According to studies, a newborn girl is the physiological equivalent of a 4- to 6-week-old boy.
- According Dr. William S. Pollock in the Department of psychiatry at Harvard medical school, "Although boys have the same emotional potential as girls, their emotional range is soon limited to a menu of three related feelings: rage, triumph, and lust." Anything else and they risk being seen as a sissy, says Dr. Pollack.

Male vulnerability and our need to act like "real men" can be deadly. When asked if the American man was an endangered species, Dr. Herb Goldberg, the author of *The Hazards of Being Male*, replied, "Absolutely! The male has paid a heavy price for his masculine 'privilege' and power. He is out of touch with his emotions and his body. He is playing by the rules of the male game plan and with lemming-like purpose he is destroying himself—emotionally, psychologically, and physically."

According to Vikki Stark, author of *Runaway Husbands: The Abandoned Wife's Guide to Recovery and Renewal*, "Women are shocked to learn that it is really men who are the more emotionally fragile gender. Men are far more at risk for being hurt, and when they are, they have fewer resources to deal with that pain."

2. Men long to be touched, but are afraid of their need.

Males long to be touched, loved, and nurtured, but we are afraid of it as well. Why is that? A number of studies show that mothers talk to, cuddle, and breastfeed male infants significantly less than female infants.

So boys experience a nurturing deficit from the very beginning and long to make up for what we didn't get. However, as boys get older we are taught to be tough and not to need the "tender loving care" that most girls more often get from their parents, relatives, and friends. These conflicting desires create a huge ambivalence inside most men. Inside we know we need extra nurturing. But we are told that it isn't manly to need it. If we act too "needy," we will be rejected by the very women who we long to be nurtured by. Do you get a sense of the bind we feel?

3. Touch deprived men become obsessed with sex.

For many men the only time they allow themselves to be touched is when they are having sex. When a couple is having less sex than desired, it may feel like a loss of intimacy for the woman. For the man, it feels like he is losing something vital to his survival.

4. Men often use sex to get the "mothering" they missed as children.

Men have an unconscious compulsion to get their spouse to give them the "mothering" they missed growing up. According to John W. Travis, M.D., author of *Why Men Leave,* "It's no surprise, then, that most of the unbonded boys in our culture grow into men who spend a good deal of their lives unconsciously seeking a mommy-figure to provide them with the nurturing they were denied as infants/children (fueled by advertising that prominently features the breasts they were denied.)"

5. Men's hunger for nurturing gets stronger as they age.

Many men may do all right early on in the relationship when a lot of focus is on meeting their needs. We may appear to be "perfect gentlemen" giving the woman all the signs of love she needs.

In fact, we are giving her the things we know will get us the love and care we desperately seek.

However, as the relationship matures and children are born and grow up, we increasingly lose our special position with the woman. As she matures, she expresses more of her own needs. Work and other demands make her less available. We may initially compensate for the loss by getting more involved with work, drink, drugs, or other forms escape, but deep inside a time-bomb is ticking. One little loss, a small disappointment, or threat to our stability and the whole house of cards begins to fall.

6. No matter how much love a woman gives it doesn't make up for childhood losses.

Many women feel frustrated that no matter how much love and nurture they give to the man, it never seems to be enough. The love of a good woman can never make up for the losses a man suffered growing up. But he doesn't know that. He believes that she *could, would*, and *must* give him what he needs. If she doesn't, his love suddenly turns to hate. Although he hungers for nurture and touch, he often expresses it through his desire for more sex. When he doesn't get "enough," he gets angry and mean.

From her perspective, her wonderful, loving mate has suddenly gone from Dr. Jekyll to Mr. Hyde, from Mr. Nice to Mr. Mean. From his perspective, all the love and nurture he was *promised* when he met and married his spouse, has systematically been taken away from him. He feels he's been set up and betrayed. In his mind he deserved to be treated special, that *his* needs *are* more important than anyone else's, that his spouse should want to have sex more frequently.

Unconsciously he believes that his spouse has promised to take care of him and now she's abandoning him. At this stage he may become violently angry, jealous, or withdrawn. He may see his children as competitors for his spouse's affections and criticize them for real or imagined transgressions. Outwardly he appears mean and controlling. Inwardly he is in a panic. He's like an infant who has lost his mommy and he thinks he will die.

7. Men don't leave for the reasons you think.

Most men don't leave for the reason you (or they) think. They are not leaving because they are not "in love" with you like they used to be, or because they're trying to "find themselves," or "need their space," or for the endless transgressions they may accuse you of perpetrating. These may be secondary reasons. But the primary reason men leave is that they are overwhelmed with shame. They feel ashamed that they feel so needy for love and nurture. They feel ashamed that they are acting in hurtful ways towards those they love. They feel ashamed of the rage that engulfs them. And most deeply, they feel ashamed for feeling ashamed over things that seem so trivial on the surface (I'm leaving because I don't feel the romantic attraction I did when we met 30 years ago?). They have built their manhood (and the hoped-for love and nurture they thought it would bring them) on being clear, strong and decisive. Now they feel clouded, weak, and ambivalent. The very foundation of their existence seems to be crumbling under them.

They feel they need to leave the relationship to keep the core of their identity from being destroyed. They feel they need to leave the relationship to keep from destroying the people they love the most. In their state of mind, leaving is the most kind and loving thing they can do to protect their spouse and children from the rage that is building up inside. They leave because they feel the long-repressed childhood traumas coming to the surface, which many men would rather die than confront.

So, given all of this "secret" knowledge, what can you do?

1. Let this sink in for a while.

When I tell women the truth about the secret reasons men leave, it is disorienting. It shakes the foundations of their own world, how they have come to understand their own identity as a woman, wife, and mother. It also rings true for them and a lot of what has been going on makes sense and falls into place.

2. Have compassion for yourself.

No one really knows what they are getting themselves into when they say, "I do." If we knew, perhaps fewer of us would make this kind of lifetime commitment. Or perhaps we wouldn't be so hard on ourselves when we're not able to be the kind of spouse that we dreamed we would be. Few women really understand the inner life of men, just as few men understand what really goes on inside the heart and mind of a woman. So, if you've felt inadequate to the task, have some compassion for yourself. Recognize that you have been doing the best you could and with new knowledge you'll be able to do even better.

3. Have compassion for the man.

Once you recognize how vulnerable men are and how much time they spend trying to deny their weakness and act like the men they imagine women want them to be, you can have more understanding of what's really driving him. You can let go of your negative beliefs about men—that they are arrogant, aggressive, stupid, sex-crazed, mean, etc. You can let in the reality that they are really just confused, wounded human beings doing their best to love and be loved in a world that has deprived us all of getting what we need the most.

4. Let the whole question of "staying or leaving" be held within a larger container of "How can we truly heal our wounds, nurture our relationship, and take care of each other?"

Once you know what is really going on, his desire to leave can be seen as part of the healing process. Even if he leaves, that doesn't have to be the end. Leaving can be seen as another step along the way to understanding the past, reclaiming the present, and building a new and better future.

5. Commit to working with a guide.

Because these issues are so important and the journey so new and confusing for many, I recommend you find a knowledgeable therapist or counselor to help guide you through this process. Finding the right guide isn't easy. Just because a person has the right credential doesn't mean they've been over this territory enough to guide others. Be tenacious. Be creative. Be willing to make mistakes. But never give up.

In this space you can write down your thoughts and feelings. What things made the most sense in this chapter? What things will be the easiest for you to engage? Which will be the most difficult? How committed are you to making your life and your relationship the most joyful possible?

NOTES

PART II:

UNDERSTANDING YOUR MAN

Chapter 9: Why Do So Many Mid-Life Men Turn Mean?

Dear Dr. Diamond,

I am forty-eight and have been married 26 years. I'm noticing that I am unusually cross and nasty with my wife who I love very much. It just comes out unexpectedly before I realize it. Then it is too late. I feel like apologizing, but somehow I never do. I can see the hurt in her eyes and I feel terribly guilty. I don't understand why I do this. Can you help me? JT.

Although Irritable Male Syndrome can occur at any age, it is quite prevalent at mid-life. What is it about mid-life that causes men to become angry? Why do they take it out on the person they say they love the most? These are the kinds of questions I hear from women who are trying to understand what is going on in their relationship.

In order to understand what is going on with men at mid-life, we have to recognize that mid-life is a difficult time for women as well as men. In fact, middle age is the worst time of life for most people. An international study of 2 million people from 80 nations found that men and women in their 40s were more likely to be depressed and weren't as happy as other ages. The researchers found happiness levels followed a U shaped curve, with happiness higher towards the start and end of our lives and leaving us most miserable in middle age.

Interestingly, in the U.S. they found a significant difference between men and women, with unhappiness reaching a peak at around 40 years of age for women and 50 years of age for men. I think this is one of the reasons why women are often "blindsided." The unhappiness men feel surfaces at different times than it does for women. The woman's happiness has been on the upswing for 10 years and all of a sudden her man tells her he's unhappy and wants to move out.

The researchers found the same U-shape in happiness levels and life satisfaction for 72 countries including Albania, Argentina, Australia, Iceland, Iraq, Ireland, the United States, Uzbekistan, and Zimbabwe. When asked what he thought caused this mid-life unhappiness, lead researcher Dr. Andrew Oswald from the University of Warwick in England said he wasn't sure. "My best conjecture is that people eventually learn to quell their infeasible aspirations," he says. "They manage to get their expectations into line with what they can actually achieve."

Many men feel unhappy and, not understanding why, blame their partners. It can be helpful to know that the mid-life slump in happiness may be affecting everyone and won't be solved by leaving their wives or finding another partner. "It looks from the data like something happens deep inside humans," says Dr. Oswald. "For the average person in the modern world, the dip in mental health and happiness comes on slowly, not suddenly in a single year. Only in their 50s do most people emerge from the low period. But encouragingly, by the time you are 70, if you are still physically fit then on average you are as happy and mentally healthy as a 20-year-old."

Oswald concludes with hope that if people can understand what is going on with men and women at mid-life, it might help them get through this stage without wrecking their relationship. "Perhaps realizing that such feelings are completely normal in midlife might even help individuals survive this phase better."

I tell men and women that being unhappy doesn't mean someone is to blame. Mid-life is like adolescence in that respect. Remember when we were going through puberty? We could go from very up to very down without anything happening. It helps to remember that mid-life is just a downer for many of us. Hang in there and you'll find life getting sweeter as you get older.

Don't ever let your man convince you that you are the cause of his unhappiness. I tell people, "It's your life, not your wife, that needs to be fixed."

The real causes of mid-life woes are related to the losses that many men feel and their inability to talk about them, to change what can be changed, and to accept what cannot. Not all men experience all these losses, but most men experience many of them:

- Hormone levels are dropping.
- Sexual vigor is diminishing.
- Erections are less frequent and less firm.
- The beautiful image we had of our partner when we first fell in love is replaced by one who looks much older and less attractive to us.
- Our own image of youthful vigor and physical prowess has changed to one where we see a "doddery old-man."
- Children are leaving home.
- We long to follow them, but feel trapped in a life we're not sure we chose.
- Parents are getting sick and dying.
- Job horizons are narrowing.
- Job security is gone.
- Retirement seems less and less possible.
- Friends are having their first heart attacks and cancer scares.
- Hopes and dreams are fading away.

Although mid-life men and women may both be unhappy, men more often express their unhappiness through anger. Women more often express their unhappiness through sadness. Men "act out" their pain and often blame those closest to them. Women "act in" their pain and often feel guilty and blame themselves when things go wrong in the relationship. Women are more likely to talk about the losses they are experiencing. Men tend to keep their feelings bottled up.

"How can I get him to open up and talk to me?" This is one of the most common questions I get from women. It isn't easy, I know. But here's a simple thing you can do. Go for a walk. Over the years, I've found that men are more comfortable with "side-to-side" communication, rather than communicating "face-to-face." He's more likely to open up when you're walking and you're not looking into each other's eyes.

There may be a biological basis for the different ways the sexes deal with their feelings when they are under stress. We've all heard of the stress response in which our bodies prepare us for "fight" or "flight." When a wild animal burst into the camp of our hunter-gatherer ancestors they would either fight the intruder or run for their lives. Until recently we assumed that the way men and women dealt with stress was the same.

But fight or flight is only part of a bigger picture, according to Shelley Taylor, Ph.D., a psychology professor at UCLA. Taylor and her colleagues found that stress can elicit another behavioral pattern they call "tend and befriend"—especially in females. Taylor's team found that, during tough times, *stressed* females spend significantly more time tending to vulnerable offspring than males. They also found that women reached out to female friends and relatives more.

Men, particularly as they age, have fewer close friends and have more superficial connections with family than is true for women. My wife tells me that the best thing I ever did for our marriage was joining a men's group. She believes, as do I, that the "befriending" I experience in my men's group helps keep me from being so angry around my wife.

I've also gotten much closer to my adult children as well as our grandchildren. Life can get lonelier as we age. Being involved with young people, "tending" them, not only keeps us feeling young, but it gives our lives meaning and purpose. Often mid-life men who seem mean, are hungry to be of help to others. We feel mean and ugly when we believe we don't have anything valuable to contribute. Being deeply involved with friends and family can be the most important antidote to IMS that we have.

In the following space, write down your thoughts. How do you feel when he blames you for his unhappiness? What losses has your man experienced? What losses have you experienced? As they ask in Alcoholics Anonymous recovery circles, what's helped you to accept those things that can't be changed, to change the things that you can change, and given you the wisdom to know the difference?

NOTES

NOTES

Chapter 10: Can Hormonal Changes Cause Him to Become More Irritable?

Dear Dr. Jed,

I love a wonderful man that for no "real" reason left after our being together for several years. He just fits the image you write about so perfectly. At forty-three years of age, he did a total turn around, becoming selfish, angry, forgetful, and indecisive. He says he still cares about me, but needs to find himself. The worst part is that he does not have any interest in women, not even me. He won't see a doctor. He says that nothing is wrong with him. To me he's acting "hormonal." Could that be part of the problem?

Although many people associate being "hormonal" with being female, the truth is that male hormonal changes are every bit as real and can be as troublesome as any changes that women experience. It's time we broke the silence and began talking about the fact that men, too, undergo hormonal changes throughout their lives. Here are some important things about hormones that you need to know:

1. Hormones are critical for health.

Hormones are one of the body's great communication networks (the others are the nervous and immune systems). A hormone molecule, released by one of about a dozen glands, travels through the blood until it reaches a cell with a receptor that it fits. Then, like a key in a lock, the molecule attaches to the receptor and sends a signal inside the cell. The signal may tell the cell to produce a certain protein or to multiply.

Hormones are involved in just about every biological process: immune function, reproduction, growth, even controlling other hormones. They can work at astonishingly small concentrations— in parts per billion or trillion. As Nancy Cetel, M.D., reminds us, "Hormones make the world go around."

2. Men have "female" hormones and women have "male" hormones.

When we think of female hormones we often think of *estrogen* and when we think of male hormones we often think of *testosterone*. But males make estrogen and females make testosterone. Estrogen in the male bloodstream may account for his desire, not just for sex, but for love and intimacy. Estrogen promotes receptivity and touching, qualities that both men and women value. Testosterone in the female bloodstream contributes to her sexual desire. If her testosterone level is too low, her sexual well-being will be compromised.

3. Testosterone is a vital hormone that has been misunderstood.

For most of us, hormones are a mystery and male hormones are an even bigger mystery. We know that testosterone contributes to sexual desire, but it does much more. Among other things, it signals cells to build muscle, make red blood cells, produce sperm, and release neurotransmitters in the brain. But its influence on sexuality and mood are the areas that are most important to us as we gain understanding of hormonal affects on IMS men.

Testosterone is produced by the Leydig cells of the testicles (in women, it is produced in the ovaries and the adrenal glands) and most of it is secreted into the bloodstream, traveling to locations as distant as the brain. Testosterone is an anabolic steroid. Although news stories and magazines often make *steroid* seem like a dangerous drug such as heroin, the truth is that every one of us is filled with steroids and we would be unable to live without them.

Abraham Morgentaler, M.D., Associate Clinical Professor at Harvard Medical School and author of the book *Testosterone For Life,* dispels some of the myths about testosterone:

- There is no evidence that testosterone is related to violence.
- Criminals *do not* have higher levels of testosterone than non-criminals.
- Testosterone *is* associated with healthy sexuality in males and females.

4. Although too much testosterone can cause men to become irritable, IMS is usually caused by too little testosterone.

We've heard of "roid rage" in which football players use male steroids to increase their strength and aggressiveness. Roid rage is a term given to people who act in very aggressive or hostile manner after taking large doses, usually on a regular basis, of *anabolic steroids*, sometimes nicknamed as *roids*. These steroids are similar in chemical structure to testosterone.

Although some males do use steroids to bulk up or to make them feel more positive and powerful, their use and abuse is greatly exaggerated in the press. Much more common and much less discussed is the negative effect of *too little* testosterone on men's physical and emotional well-being.

5. Low testosterone and IMS.

Dr. Gerald Lincoln, who coined the term "Irritable Male Syndrome," found that lowering levels of testosterone in his research animals caused them to become more irritable, biting their cages as well as the researchers who were testing them. Low testosterone also has a negative affect on men.

Although low testosterone is more prevalent in men over 40, it can occur in men of any age. The following questionnaire, developed by John E. Morley at St. Louis University School of Medicine, can give a pretty good indication of whether a man's testosterone levels are too low. Answer the following questions:

1. Do you have a decrease in libido (sex drive)?
2. Do you have a lack of energy?
3. Do you have a decrease in strength and/or endurance?
4. Have you lost height?
5. Have you noticed a decreased "enjoyment of life?"
6. Are you sad and/or grumpy?
7. Are your erections less strong?
8. Have you noticed a recent deterioration in your ability to play sports?
9. Are you falling asleep after dinner?
10. Has there been a recent deterioration in your work.

If you answered "yes" to questions 1 or 7 and "yes" to any three other questions, there is evidence that you are suffering from testosterone deficiency. To confirm whether your testosterone is low you need to have a blood test done.

6. Getting the right blood tests.

As Dr. Morgentaler says, "There are so many blood tests to measure testosterone that it is no wonder most physicians are

confused about which ones to order and how to interpret them."
As a result you may have to educate your own doctor to insure
you are getting the best advice and support. Here are Dr. Morgentaler's recommendations:

If you think your man may have low T, he should have two
blood tests done:

- Total T
- Free T

Total T measures the total amount of testosterone in the bloodstream, while Free T measures the amount that is not bound to a
carrier molecule. It is this Free T that is available to give the body
what it needs. "If either one is low (Total T less than 350 ng/dl
and, especially, free T less than 15 pg/ml, then there is a strong
possibility that he has low T and might benefit from treatment."

Many doctors are not familiar with hormone testing. I have
found that a good place to learn more and get your hormone levels
tested is through ZRT laboratory. ZRT's founder and director, Dr.
David Zava is one of the experts in the field. And best of all they
will send you everything you need through the mail. Check out
their website at: *www.ZRTlab.com.*

7. Treatment options for low testosterone.

Fortunately, there are many options available for treating low
testosterone:

DIETARY

- Lose weight—"Being as little as 10 pounds overweight," says
  hormone expert Larrian Gillespie, M.D., "can increase estrogen
  levels in men and decrease testosterone levels."
- Drink less—"Alcohol has a direct toxic effect on the testicles
  and can lower testosterone concentrations in men even if they
  don't drink chronically," says Dr. Gillespie.

EXERCISE

Although unlikely to contribute to large changes in testosterone levels, exercise has been shown, in some studies, to increase
testosterone levels. Along with diet it can contribute to health and
well-being.

TESTOSTERONE RESTORATION

Testosterone restoration remains controversial. Many doctors are not familiar with the latest research and others are fearful about possible adverse effects including prostate cancer. Dr. Morgentaler has been offering testosterone restoration treatments for more than 30 years. Here's what he says, "Even after all these years of working with men with low T, I continue to be amazed at the ways in which T therapy can absolutely change a man's life."

WHAT YOU CAN DO

1. Learn all you can about IMS and Andropause.

In understanding the male change of life, we are 40 years behind in our knowledge and understanding compared to what we know about women. My books *Surviving Male Menopause* and *The Irritable Male Syndrome* can help you learn more. I also recommend, *The Testosterone Revolution* by Malcolm Carruthers, M.D. and *Testosterone for Life* by Abraham Morgentaler, M.D. Since men and women often go through "the change" at the same time, you'll want to read, *Double Menopause: What to Do When Both You and Your Mate Go through Hormonal Changes Together* by Nancy Cetel, M.D.

2. Understand your man's shame about "losing his manhood."

For most men, the thought that he may be losing hormonal health or sexual function raises horrible pictures of "impotency" and "loss of manhood." Don't be surprised if he is reluctant to discuss these issues.

3. Let him "discover" the information on his own.

Although most men are reluctant to talk about loss of libido or low testosterone, they want to have better sex and love lives. When men discovered there was a blue pill that could bring back their erections, they talked to their doctors on their own (usually with more than a little support from their wives).

If he seems reluctant to talk, leave the book out where he'll find it on his own. Dr. Carruthers calls Viagra and testosterone, "the dynamic duo." If your man liked the one, he may love knowing about both.

Use this space to discuss your own thoughts on hormones and IMS. Do you think that there may be a relationship between IMS and hormonal imbalances in your man? Do you think your man may have low testosterone? While recognizing that this may be a sensitive area for your man, are you willing to encourage him to get his hormone levels checked? At ZRT laboratory, you can get both "his" and "hers" hormone checks. Would you consider having your own hormone levels checked as well?

NOTES

Chapter 11: Can a Man Have Irritable Male Syndrome *and* Male Menopause?

Dear Dr. Diamond,

I only wished I could have learned about Male Menopause sooner. You see, for the past two years he has had all the symptoms mentioned in your book. I had no idea what was going on. He kept complaining about being so lonely even though I was always there for him. I knew how he felt about his looks and his idea of staying "forever young." He bought a new Harley, but it was never fast enough, and he went to Sturgis for the bike rallies, but it didn't seem to satisfy him as it once had. He became more and more angry and I got angry back at him. I finally threw him out of the house...He died a year later. I know it wasn't my fault, but I just wish I had better understood what was going on. SH

When I began the research for my book, *Male Menopause,* I was skeptical about the concept itself. I had been a therapist for over thirty years and had worked with thousands of mid-life men and women. Most of the women who were approaching menopause experienced marked changes that were related to physiological and hormonal shifts in body chemistry.

It was clear to me that something was also going on with the men, but I assumed that men's changes were more psychological than physical. I had heard a number of men and women talk about "male menopause," but wondered if they were just complaining about the difficulties of being a man or trying to justify their irresponsible mid-life behavior. In a society where more and more people see themselves as victims—"my hormones made me do it"—it is not a surprising excuse.

As a therapist I have little tolerance for men (or women) who bemoan their lives or who blame their bad behavior on someone or something other than themselves. However, after completing ten years of research I concluded that mid-life men have significant hormonal and physiological changes as they move from the first half of life to the second.

There seem to be two major groups of clinicians addressing issues of male menopause or andropause. One group believes it is a myth. "There is no such thing as 'male menopause.' Men are just getting older and there is no need to do anything," this group asserts. The other group believes that male menopause or andropause is real, but it is simply due to a loss of testosterone. "Restore a man's testosterone levels and his symptoms go away," this group responds. I'm part of a more select group of clinicians who believes that male menopause is real, but that these changes are due to more than just hormonal fluctuations and include psychological, physiological, interpersonal, sexual, social, and spiritual changes.

HOW DO I KNOW IF HE IS GOING THROUGH MALE MENOPAUSE OR IMS?

Those who have heard about my research on Irritable Male Syndrome and Male Menopause want to know how they can tell which problem is affecting their man. It can be confusing since the symptoms overlap. Here's how you can tell. First, take the IMS quiz to determine whether your man has IMS (See Chapter 18, How Do I Know If He Has IMS?) Second, check his birth certificate. If he's between the ages of 40 and 60, he has Male Menopause as well.

DO MEN REALLY GO THROUGH "MALE MENOPAUSE?"

The term "male menopause," of course is a misnomer. Men don't have a menstrual cycle and so don't stop having one. The correct clinical term is "andropause." However, there are enough similarities between what women and men go through that the term "male menopause" is a useful one.

Here are some things you should know:

1. Male menopause begins with hormonal, physiological, and chemical changes that occur in all men generally between the ages of 40 and 60, though it can occur as early as 35 or as late as 65 in some men.

2. These changes affect all aspects of a man's life. Male menopause is, thus, a physical condition with psychological, interpersonal, social, and spiritual dimensions.

3. What we call the "mid-life" crisis encompasses the psychological, interpersonal, and social aspects of male menopause.

4. Puberty is a stage that all of us go through and marks the transition between childhood and adulthood. Male menopause is the transition between adulthood and what I call "super-adulthood." For some going through puberty is relatively painless. While for others it is quite difficult. The same is true for men going through male menopause.

5. Rather than being the beginning of the end as many men fear, it is really the end of the beginning. If understood and addressed directly, male menopause can be the passage to the most passionate, powerful, productive, and purposeful time of a man's life.

6. In our initial study of 1,000 men between the ages of 35 and 65 who came to our clinic with concerns about health, major symptoms included:

    - Irritability and anger in 85%
    - Reduced libido or potency in 82%
    - Fatigue or loss of vitality in 80%
    - Marital conflict in 75%
    - Weight gain in 70%
    - Depression in 65%
    - Dissatisfaction with present life in 60%
    - Economic worries in 60%
    - Night-sweats or hot flashes in 50%

These are higher percentages than those found in the general population, but they indicate the kinds of issue that men who are having difficulties may experience.

IRRITABLE MALE SYNDROME, MALE MENOPAUSE, AND ADOLESCENCE

Anyone who has watched a boy become a young man has seen the symptoms of the Irritable Male Syndrome. One day he is a sweet, caring child. Overnight, it seems, he turns into a monster. He becomes irritable and angry, sullen and remote. He withdraws into his computer and cell phone, lost in a world we don't understand and can't join. When he interacts with us at all, he can bite off our heads at the slightest provocation. Nothing we do is ever right; nothing seems to comfort his restless spirit. Yet there are times, we see the son we remembered—kind, sweet, and understanding. We think the person we loved has returned and our hearts open, only to be dashed by his latest round of angry accusations and sullen withdrawal. Sound familiar?

If we have experienced an adolescent male, we know the signs, and we know he will soon—though not soon enough if we are living in the same house—grow up. But read the above description again and ask yourself, is this the behavior of a 15-year-old or a 50-year-old?

I often call male menopause, "adolescence the second time around," because they are similar in many ways. Both are transition periods. In the case of adolescence, it is the transition between childhood and adulthood. With male menopause, it is the transition between first adulthood and second adulthood or super-adulthood. Although Irritable Male Syndrome can occur at any age, it most common age range is between 15 and 25 and between 40 and 55, during these two major life-phase transitions.

WHAT YOU CAN DO

1. Remember this is a life stage, not a death sentence.

When IMS overlaps with male menopause it can seem like our whole life is falling apart. Little problems turn into huge ones. It can seem like life is just going down hill. Many men begin to feel hopeless and think the only solution is to leave. Many women feel overwhelmed and believe the only solution is to leave. Remembering this is a life-stage that he will come through, can help you keep a positive perspective.

2. When he says mean things, remember it is the adolescent in him talking.

If you've raised adolescents, you'll remember the times they told you they hated you, and said and did things that wounded you deeply. However, over time you learned not to become invested in their angry outbursts. You didn't dissolve when they told you how awful you were and they'd be much happier if you were out of their lives. You remembered that this was a stage they would pass through. You didn't take it personally. You need to remember this now. Repeat over and over, "This is a stage he is going through. He may believe I am the cause of all his problems, but I'm not. This too shall pass."

Admittedly, this is much more difficult when your husband is acting like an adolescent than it is when it is your son. It can be terrifying when he pulls away, particularly if there's another woman involved. But anything you can do to reduce the terror will help you move forward in a healthy and self-caring way.

3. Stand up for yourself and encourage him to expand his focus.

Although using a direct approach with some men, may not work, it doesn't mean you need to roll over and just take his abuse.... You might try saying: "You've got male menopause, your hormones are out of whack, and you're probably depressed. Get off my back and get help." Sometimes it's just the kind of wake up call he needs. On the other hand you might try a more indirect approach. "I know I'm going through difficult changes and I'm not the easiest to live with, but you're not so easy being around either. I know you love me, want what's best for me, and care about our relationship and our family. Would you be willing to come with me to see a counselor who can help us get through these changes together?" Of course, you'd use your own words, but you get the idea.

In the following space, write down your thoughts. Do you think your man is experiencing IMS and Male Menopause? What are the main symptoms? Does he seem to be acting like an adolescent? What things can you do that might help?

NOTES

NOTES

Chapter 12: He Has Everything He's Always Wanted. Why Is He So Unsatisfied and Angry?

Dear Dr. Diamond,

I love a wonderful man that for no "real" reason, left after we'd spent twenty-eight years building what I thought was a near perfect life together. We have three grown children who we love dearly and we'd been making plans to travel together and see all the places we said we wanted to visit before we got too old. In the last few years he's told me, repeatedly, he has everything he wants. But all of a sudden he says he's not happy. I'm totally in shock. How can he have everything he wants and be unhappy?

We've had our ups and downs like everyone, but we've always supported each other in everything we do. We own a business that we have enjoyed and it gives us an income that most people would envy. We built our "dream house" a few years ago and I thought we had it all. Now it's all falling to pieces and the worst part is I don't even know why.

If I have to move on without him, I at least want to understand what happened. Can you help? FS

There are four common experiences that are most difficult for women dealing with IMS men:

1. The whip-lash-producing turn-around that the men make. One minute they say they are happy and satisfied. The next minute they say they are unhappy and want to leave.
2. When asked what has changed, what they're unhappy about, or what would make them happy, the men shrug and say, "I don't know."
3. In bewilderment the women press for answers. And the men get more frustrated, angry, and yes, mean.

4. Many of these men seem to be the most successful. They have it all. Yet they're still unsatisfied and unhappy.

For many women it's like waking up one morning and finding yourself in an Alice-in-Wonderland world. Nothing makes any sense. Everything has turned up-side-down. You are bewildered, confused, and frightened. For some it's even worse than that. You seem to have stumbled into a "madhouse" and your formerly loving partner has turned into a crazed madman. Does any of this ring true for you?

To help women and men understand what's really going on, I introduce this short phrase that speaks to a deeper truth: *It isn't your wife that's the problem. It's your life.* Though simple, this isn't an easy concept to get across. Why is that?

1. Women and men see the cause of problems differently.

When something is wrong in their relationship or in their lives, women tend to look inside. They often ruminate, and go over and over questions like, "What did I do wrong? What's the matter with me? How can I make him happy?" Be alert for this and try to avoid blaming yourself for his problems or assuming responsibility for them.

Men, on the other hand, tend to seek for the cause of problems outside themselves. They don't usually chew on a problem. They quickly look for the cause then try to fix it. Searching for some understanding of what's making them so unhappy, they focus on the one closest to them, their wife.

2. The partner often becomes the scapegoat for the man's unhappiness.

As described in the bible, the high priest placed his hands on the head of a goat and confessed the sins of the people of Israel. The goat was then led away into the wilderness to perish, bearing the sins of the people with it. The word "scapegoat" has come to mean a person, often innocent, who is blamed and punished for the sins, crimes, or sufferings of others, generally as a way of distracting attention from the real causes.

The age-old phenomenon of scapegoating shows up everywhere. Scapegoats are found in almost every social context: in school playgrounds, in families, in small groups, and in large organizations. Whole nations may be scapegoated.

Women, throughout history, have often become the scapegoats of insecure men. From the Inquisition, when women were targeted as witches, to Rush Limbaugh's labeling women as *feminazis,* women have had to stand up against oppression.

3. Men's fear of women often comes out as anger.

When dealing with an angry IMS male, it may not be obvious to the woman (or the man) that his anger covers a terrifying fear. Most women are surprised when I suggest this. "How can he be afraid of me," they want to know. "He has all the power." Though he may, in fact, have power in some aspects of the relationship, in the emotional realm, he may feel quite powerless.

I remember a time when my first wife and I were having difficulties in our marriage. It was one of the times when I was the most nasty and mean. I didn't want to be that way and would not have admitted I was. If confronted I would have said it was my wife who was being mean by withholding her love and I was just reacting to her.

I could see that my behavior was driving her away, which scared me to death, though I wouldn't admit it. The more I tried to keep her close, the more she pulled away, and the more fearful and angry I became. This was also a time when I was the most stressed at work. I had recently lost one job and was afraid I was going to lose my current position. I wasn't sleeping and I was eating and drinking too much. I wanted to reach out to my wife, tell her how afraid I was, and cry in her arms. The very thought that I might do that terrified me. The more afraid I became, the more frustrated and irritable I got.

In his book, *Misogyny: The Male Malady,* anthropology professor David D. Gilmore, makes a profound and disturbing observation. "That men love and hate women simultaneously and in equal measure, that most men need women desperately, and that most men reject this driving need as both unworthy and dangerous."

Obviously this isn't the case of *all* men. Though this ambivalence is played out in all societies, individual men differ in the degree to which it affects them. For some of us the fear and rage are extreme. For others, we control it well and it seeps out only at times of change and stress.

We love our spouse for what they can give us, but are also frightened at the degree of our dependency. "So man must cling helplessly to woman as a shipwrecked sailor to a lifeboat in choppy seas," says Gilmore. "He desperately needs her as his salvation from all want and from oblivion; his dependency is total and desperate. But, and here's the rub, man must also separate from woman to achieve anything at all. "

Gilmore concludes with this insightful summary of the bind men feel: "And of course this powerful double-sided fixation creates a concomitant fear: the fear of abandonment, loss, withdrawal, disillusionment, and failure in life's most precious endeavors. Fraught with images of defeat, despair, and death, the fear of abandonment leads to regressive depression, panic, guilt, self-doubt, and ultimately to the rage of the thrall. The impotent rage leads to aggression; and aggression, in turn, needs a scapegoat."

All this, of course, goes on outside our awareness. These universal, epic battles are fought in the darkest parts of our psyches. All we "know" is that our spouse seems to be cold and withholding. She won't give us what we need. She seems to go out of her way to irritate us. *If* we're irritable, and it's a big *if* at the beginning, we're sure the cause lies somewhere outside ourselves. To think otherwise would bring up fears too difficult to confront.

So how do you deal with a man who pulls you close then pushes you away, who loves you one minute and hates you the next? Here are some things I have found that work:

1. Remind yourself over and over that, "I'm not the cause of his unhappiness."

Many women fall into the trap of blaming themselves. "If he has everything he could possible want and he is still miserable, I must be the cause of this problems." And of course the man telling you over and over that you *are* to blame doesn't make it easy to resist. But resist you must, for your sake and for his.

2. Lovingly stand up for yourself and refuse to be the scapegoat.

When we're afraid, we either allow ourselves to get rolled over or we strike back in anger. This is a time to send out a lot of love.

Remember this is a man who is frightened, vulnerable, and panicked. You can feel empathy for his pain. But you can also stand your ground. You can say something like this: "Look I know you are angry and upset. You have a perfect right to be given all that has happened. I'm sure I've contributed to some of your pain. I do my best, but I'm not perfect. But there are a lot of other things going on in your life. The problems aren't all connected to me. And regardless of what part I may have played, I don't deserve to be yelled at or ridiculed (or whatever IMS behavior he is exhibiting). I love you and we need to work this out together. Don't make me the enemy. I'm on your side." You may have to keep giving this message many times before it sinks in. But don't give up. Stick with it.

3. Understand the true source of happiness.

Most of us, particularly men, have been raised with the belief that having more money, and the things that money can buy, will make us happy. Our whole culture is built on the belief that we must work hard to buy more of the things that are for sale in our department stores so that we will feel good about ourselves.

Yet, research continues to show that success of this kind does not lead to greater happiness. Researchers found that pursuing and even reaching self-centered, materialist goals actually *hurt* well-being. Despite their accomplishments, people who made lots of money, transformed their appearances or became well-known, felt more *negative* emotions, like shame and anger. They also had more physical symptoms of anxiety - such as headaches, stomachaches, and loss of energy.

The people who valued close relationships, community involvement and physical health—hit the jackpot! They experienced a deeper sense of well-being, and had higher self-esteem. They also had better relationships and fewer signs of stress.

We need to recognize that a lot of the pain men experience at midlife is because they feel misled and betrayed. They were told that working long hours, making money, and buying nice things for their family would make them feel like a success. But they find out it has not.

They need to be appreciated and honored for what they have accomplished, but helped to let go of their old patterns and encouraged to put more time and energy into finding the sources of true happiness. They need time to explore, time to listen to their soul's calling, time to stop working and start living. They need find out what really matters in life and what they can give to themselves, to others, and to the world. This is a process that we each need to find for ourselves. Women can't do it for the men. They need to find the source of true happiness themselves.

Use this space to write your thoughts. What resonated with you in this chapter? In what ways has your man projected his own pain outward and blamed you for his problems? What actions are you planning to take with the information you learned here?

NOTES

Chapter 13: Why Do Mid-Life Men Want to Leave Perfectly Good Relationships?

Dear Dr. Jed,

My husband, Barry, is a 42 year-old attorney who is very successful, good looking, and very physically fit. I have to say our relationship has been close to being perfect. He pursued me in college and we got married after graduation. We have been married 19 years, with 18 1/2 of those being wonderful and blissful. He even said just 7 months ago, "You still turn me on after all these years" and "you don't need to wear makeup, you're beautiful just the way you are." We have 2 great kids, a 15 year old daughter and a 10 year old son. He has been the IDEAL husband and father for all these years...until now.

Now he says he's not sure he wants to be married and is thinking of leaving. I just can't understand it. It would make sense if he's been unhappy and there have been problems in the relationship. I know a number of couples who I think would be better off apart. But not us—it's crazy. How can a man who has everything he wants and tells me how beautiful I am and how grateful he is to be married, do a complete turn around and want to leave? LH

One of the most devastating experiences we have is to be told our mate wants to leave. It's even more painful when we didn't see it coming. And it can be downright crazy-making when it comes from a mate who seemed to be perfectly happy only "moments" before. Though I hear most often from heterosexual women, similar dynamics are present with gay and lesbian couples I've worked with. What's going on here?

Certainly one possibility is that these aren't good marriages at all. Many relationships deteriorate through time, yet one or both partners are oblivious to the unhappiness and pain that their spouse is experiencing. There are marriages that should have ended long ago, but the couple stays together because they're

78

afraid to leave. However, some other marriages are really quite healthy, though all relationships of any length have their ups and downs, yet one spouse feels suddenly driven to leave.

Why do so many men leave their partners after 15, 20, or 30 years of marriage? The couple has often weathered many of the stresses of raising children, developing financial security, and seems to be ready to enjoy their later years. Yet, just when things appear to be going well, the man becomes increasingly restless and wants to move out.

One minute the marriage is solid and he's madly in love. The next minute he's got one foot out the door. His reasons are often vague and confusing. "I just need to find myself," or "I need my space."

Linda, who wrote the letter at the beginning of the chapter, got a deeper insight into her husband after she kept pushing him to tell her what was wrong. "Finally we had a heated discussion that lasted well into the night and early morning," she told me. "Through the hours that we talked he blurted out, 'I've always been someone's son, someone's husband, someone's father. I feel like I've lost myself. When will it be my turn to have what I want?' I was shocked to hear what he said. I had no idea he wasn't happy with the things he was doing."

Linda's reaction is understandable and no doubt familiar to millions of women who have heard words like the following:

- "I love you, but I'm not *in love* with you."
- "I need to find myself."
- "I just need my space."
- "When will it be *my* turn to have what *I* want?"

What is a woman to do? Here are things I've found will work.

1. Take a step back and deal with the shock.

When a man first tells the woman what he's really thinking, it feels like she's been punched in the gut. Your mind goes blank and it's difficult to breathe. The first thing you need to do is take a step back and let some of the shock wear off. Sometimes you need to be alone, but most often it helps to be with someone you care about and who cares about you. This can be a trusted friend or family member.

Don't try to "figure things out" yet. Just tell them what he said and how you feel. "I called up my friend, Sheila," a 57-year-old woman told me. "I blurted out that Don just told me out of the blue that he wants to move out. I told her I was shocked, wounded, and confused. That's all I could say before I broke into tears. She came right over and spent the rest of the afternoon just listening to me. After a week of crying on and off and talking with friends, I feel I'm at least back in my body again."

2. Write a letter expressing your feelings and needs.

Shock numbs us and keeps us from being overwhelmed by our feelings when we experience a traumatic event. Once we have dealt with the shock, we need to allow our feelings to flow again. John Gray, author of *Men are from Mars, Women are from Venus,* developed a feeling exercise which I have adapted and have found very helpful.

Get out some paper, sit down, and write a letter to the IMS man you are dealing with. You're not going to actually send the letter or even share it with him at this time. This is for you. Once the numbness wears off, most people are feeling angry and hurt. Usually one feeling will predominate at any given time. Let's start with anger.

You simply begin, *Dear _____* (fill in his name). Let yourself express anger and blame in whatever words best fit your feelings. Don't hold back or censor yourself. Remember no one will see this other than you. Here are some words to get you started to express *anger and blame.*

> I hate it when...
> You're a real SOB and...
> I'm fed up with...
> Etc. And I need... (e.g. respect, care, understanding, etc.)

When you've gotten out some of your anger and blame, you'll begin to feel some of the hurt and pain. (If you start with hurt and pain, you'll begin to feel the anger.) Here are some words to help you express *hurt and sadness.*

> I feel so sad that you...
> I feel terribly hurt when...
> I feel sick that...
> I'm deeply disappointed because...
> Etc. And I need... (e.g. support, nurturing, kindness, etc.)

Underneath the anger and blame, hurt and sadness, you'll find feelings of *fear and insecurity.*

I'm afraid that...

I'm worried I won't be able to...

I feel scared because...

Etc. And I need... (e.g. assurance, something I can count on, someone who cares about me, etc.)

Underneath the fear and insecurity you'll find feelings of *guilt and shame.*

I feel awful that...

I didn't mean to...

I'm sorry that...

I feel ashamed about...

Etc. And I need... (e.g. forgiveness, acceptance, healing, etc.)

Finally, underneath the guilt and shame is *understanding and love.*

I understand that...

I realize now that...

I love you because...

I accept that...

I hope we can...

Etc. And I need... (e.g. time to work things out, to find ways to move ahead, ways to heal the wounds, etc.)

At the end of the letter, sign your name and write the date, and keep in a safe place. The more you write the "feeling letter," the more healing occurs. Some people find, at the beginning, it helps to write many each day. Most of us can express some of these feelings but have difficulty expressing others. Try to write something for each of the feelings listed: anger and blame, hurt and sadness, fear and insecurity, guilt and shame, understanding and love.

3. Remember it isn't over until it's over for you.

When a man says that he's leaving, the response is often one of resignation. "Well, if he's going to leave, there's nothing I can do. I'll just have to accept it." But that's not the case. First, you have to remember that no matter what he says, this is a confusing time he is going through. You have to ask yourself if you want it to be over. If the answer is "no," then you need to keep your focus on making things work out, no matter what he does.

There may come a time when you decide it's better if you go your separate ways. But don't let what he says or does, push you into agreeing with something that isn't right for you. Remind yourself, "I know he says he wants to leave, but I still want things to work out and I'm going to do everything I can to bring that about." Set a check-in date for yourself. It may be a month ahead, six-months, a year, whatever is right for you. Check in with your-self then and make a decision based on how you feel at that time.

4. Resist the temptation to resist.

When a man indicates he wants to leave, the temptation is to resist. This can be in the form of endless questions. "Why do you want to do this? What's the matter? What have I done wrong?" etc. It's easy to believe that if you could just get to the bottom of things, you could change his mind. Or resistance can be in the form of giving reasons why he should stay. "I love you. Think of the kids. We've been happy all these years. You'll be sorry." It seems that if you could just get him to see all the good things, he'll change his mind.

It doesn't work. The more you resist, the more he pulls away. A better strategy is to take care of yourself and go with his flow. Take the position that, "I can see you're unhappy and I want you to have what you need." Don't fight him. Suggest that he might be right. "Maybe that's for the best. Perhaps I'm not the right one for you." This is a good time to evaluate the relationship yourself. Is it meeting your needs? What would you like to see changed to make it better for you? Refusing to resist can be disarming. If you don't challenge him, he will begin to challenge himself. He'll start to question whether leaving is what he really wants.

5. Make your life so good you'll be happy whether he stays or leaves.

When we've built a life with another person, the loss of that life feels devastating. But since you haven't given up, you can take this time to make your life as full as it can be. Deepen your friend-ships, make new friends, expand your work in the world, go on an adventure. You get the idea. You want to make your life so full and fun, he'll reconsider what he might lose if he leaves. If your life is full and getting fuller, at some point you might decide you don't really want a guy who is unhappy, depressed, and lacks the desire to build a life with you. Make your life so wonderful that sharing it with him is a real joy. But also make it so wonderful that a life without him can feel fine as well.

Use this space to write down the things that really make your life meaningful. What things are you prepared to do to make your life wonderful whether he stays or leaves?

NOTES

Chapter 14: How Can A Man Change From *Dr. Jekyll* to *Mr. Hyde* Seemingly Overnight?

Dear Dr. Jed,

My husband's personality suddenly changed from my funny, loving Dr. Jekyll into an angry, resentful, and controlling Mr. Hyde. He grew increasingly angry with me and seemed to withdraw from our marriage. We used to enjoy being together. Now he spends most of his time in his home office or at the neighborhood bars until well after

1 A.M. Simultaneously, he was constantly criticizing me for the things he once used to compliment me on. He treated me like a child in a crowded store, scolding me in public for bumping into someone who, instead, walked into me.

When I expressed a desire to go back to school and then work, he said that he didn't understand why I couldn't be happy staying home doing housework all day. Since it was an every day exercise in futility, I just couldn't be happy staying home, especially if I was going to be slapped in the face with a bunch of criticism and anger. What's going on here? BK.

When I finished my research on the changes I was seeing in men and the women who loved them, I almost named the book *The Jekyll and Hyde Syndrome* instead of *The Irritable Male Syndrome*. The latter speaks more to the emotional state that men begin to exhibit. The first title speaks to the transformation that occurs and the change of personality that so many men exhibit. Let's look more closely at what's going on.

The book *Dr. Jekyll and Mr. Hyde* was written by Robert Louis Stevenson in 1886 and has become a mainstay of stage and screen throughout the world. It seems to speak to something in the human psyche, particularly the male mind. The story is about Dr. Henry Jekyll who is pursuing his life-long quest to separate the two natures of man to get at the essence of good and evil.

Refused help by his peers and superiors, he begins experiments on himself with his own formula. He meets with success, yet the results are shocking. The evil nature of Dr. Jekyll surfaces as a separate identity: Edward Hyde. Hyde begins murdering the members of the Board of Governors who previously refused assistance to Jekyll's cause. Throughout the story Jekyll fights in vain to keep his darker half under control.

Even this short summary of the story can give us important insights about what is going on with so many men today. Like the good doctor in the story, men today are questioning what is "right" and what is "wrong" in the world. For many men, they have spent their lives trying to do what they thought was right. They've done their best to make the world a better place for their wives and children, but they feel they have failed.

Many have worked at jobs that no longer exist or have been laid off because of a sinking economy. More and more men, whether working or not, feel that their dreams of success are slipping away from them. They work harder and make less money. They do everything they can to create a secure life for themselves and their family and see their retirement and savings accounts getting lower and lower. Their fear, frustration, and shame often turn to anger.

Another aspect of the story is instructive. Dr. Jekyll feels betrayed by his superiors, and as the transformed Mr. Hyde he begins to murder the Board of Governors who refused previously to support his efforts. Susan Faludi, author of *Stiffed: The Betrayal of the American Male* captures the betrayal felt by the average guy towards the men in power who promised that if he played by the rules and worked hard he would ascend the ladder of success until he reached the top. "Implicit in all of this," says Faludi, "was a promise of loyalty, a guarantee to the new man of tomorrow that his company would never fire him, his wife would never leave him, and the team he rooted for would never pull up stakes. Instead, the average man found his father was an absent father, the job market had no place for him, women were ashamed of his inability to make a decent living, and his favorite sports team moved to another city and abandoned him."

The first step to helping yourself and the man in your life is to put yourself in his shoes. Can you empathize with how a man feels? Can you experience the rage that comes from the betrayal of a promise? Can you understand why Dr. Jekyll becomes Mr. Hyde and goes after those in power who betrayed him?

"I can understand why he might feel betrayed by his employers, or even the whole economic system that this country is based on, but why does he take it out on me?" one woman asked me in frustration and despair. "I'm on his side. I've stood by him. It's not fair that somehow I've turned into the bad guy."

I can truly empathize with women who feel this way. It isn't right and it isn't fair. But it's often how things are. So what is a woman to do?

<u>1. You need to overcome the shock of feeling your man has been stolen and replaced by a monster who might kill you in your sleep.</u>

Most women go into shock when it seems that kind, understanding, Dr. Jekyll has turned into cold, mean Mr. Hyde. Whether your man is just a little irritable lately or he has become hurtful, he has not been forever transformed into a monster.

To break the cycle of shock and fear you need to say something like this to yourself: "I'm feeling stunned and frightened at my man's change of behavior because I need to feel secure and loved. I don't know exactly what's going on, but I know he's a good man and we can get to the bottom of what's bothering him and find the care and connection we both desire." Recognizing what is going on, without imagining that your man is lost forever, can help calm your fears, particularly in the early stages of recovery.

<u>2. Talk to friends and family who support you, your man, and your relationship.</u>

Many women feel ashamed of their husband's behavior and try to keep it a secret from friends and family. This is the time to reach out to others and tell them what's going on and how you're feeling. Let them know you want to do everything you can to take care of yourself, take care of your man, to care for your relationship and your family.

Don't fall into the trap of blaming yourself for his bad behavior or the trap of blaming him. Some women talk to friends who have become down on men, and end up working themselves into a frenzy of "bad-mouth the bastard." This may help you feel better, temporarily, but will likely break up your relationship, not heal it. Seek support from those who feel things can get worked out, not from those who want you to get out. But also be sure you are receiving support to set strong boundaries against being abused.

3. Make a commitment to helping yourself, your man, and the relationship and set a date to re-examine the commitment.

Some women abandon a troubled relationship too soon, without working hard enough to repair it. However, many women stay in a destructive relationship long after they have done everything possible to make it better.

Making a commitment for improvement, and setting a date to check in, will focus your attention on the positive changes you hope to bring about. It will also give you a specific time to re-examine your commitment and see if things are changing for the better. "It was really helpful to make a time-specific commitment," one woman told me. "It really helped me feel more confident and less panicked. I had a goal of making things better, but I also knew I wouldn't stay forever in a bad situation that wasn't improving."

4. Protect yourself from violence.

Many women become so committed to their man, their family, and their relationship they neglect taking care of themselves. Let's be clear. Some IMS men can become aggressive and even violent. The best way to protect yourself is to plan ahead. You don't have to anticipate violence, but you must be clear with yourself what you will do should it occur.

You need to say to yourself, "I may love this man and be committed to the relationship, but I won't let myself be harmed if he becomes violent." Most of us have a "gut" feeling when someone is about to become violent. We need to respect that intuition. If you feel his anger escalating, you must do whatever it takes to be sure you are safe and protected. You may need to get out of the house and stay away for a few hours, or even a few days. You should have friends or family you can stay with if need be. Leaving the house to keep yourself safe doesn't necessarily mean you are leaving the relationship.

Many women are afraid to leave, because they think he will get even more violent. If violence is an issue, you must get yourself to a safe place first. Then you can reassure him and begin to make things better. You can talk to him on the phone or send him a letter or e-mail saying something like, "I care about you and I want more than anything for us to work things out so we can both feel good about ourselves, each other, and the relationship. I'm not leaving permanently. I just needed some time to get myself together and feel safe. And I think you needed some time to cool off. Maybe we could find some outside help, but I truly believe that we can work things out. Let's work together to get through this."

5. You need to build up your own self-esteem.

Irritable male syndrome can cause men to become more aggressive, cold, and mean. It can cause women to become more withdrawn, tearful, and guilty. You may need to put special effort into building yourself back up. "During the last few years with my husband, my self-esteem has gone down and down," a 44-year-old woman explained to me. "I tell myself not to believe all the unkind things he says about me, but they seem to sink into my subconscious no matter what I do. I've never seen myself as a fearful person, but my nerves are on edge and my stomach tightens up whenever he comes into the room. I feel hurt by what he says to me and then I get down on myself because I let what he says hurt me."

Talk to yourself. Remind yourself of all your good qualities. Write in a journal. Put down something you like about your physical appearance. Describe something that you feel good about accomplishing. And write down a personality trait that you like. Spend time with people who value you and ask them to tell you what they like about you.

Use this space to write in. What Jekyll and Hyde changes have you seen in your man? What betrayals are you feeling? Take some time to write down what you want and need in this relationship and some ways that might be possible.

NOTES

NOTES

Chapter 15: My Brother is Gay and Has All The Symptoms of IMS. Is There Help For Him?

Dear Dr. Jed,

My brother, David, has been in a long-term relationship with his partner, Bryce. They've been together for 22 years and have one of the best relationships of any couple I know. Our families are close and my husband and I often have them over for dinner. Things seemed to be fine and we were having our usual banter about politics, nothing heated, just four educated people discussing the state of the world.

Evidently something was said and David launched into a verbal tirade, accusing Bryce of "being an apologist for those right-wing crazies." Everyone was shocked. Bryce is as liberal as they come and David is usually easy-go-lucky. Later, David went for a walk and Bryce told us that David "hasn't been himself" lately. "He's been having stress at work, which isn't new for him, but he's been bringing it home. I try and be as loving and understanding as I can", Bryce said, "but he seems to see me as the 'bad guy.' He's become hypersensitive. If I leave a towel on the counter, he gets irritated. If I don't clean up a spill to his satisfaction, he makes me feel like I'm a slob."

Their relationship is one that most people admire and wish to emulate. But this IMS stuff, if that's what it is, could tear it apart. I've always been able to talk to David. He'd open up to me when he wouldn't with anyone else. But he's shut down and I don't know how to reach him. TC.

While there are some differences between gay men and straight men, irritable male syndrome isn't one of them. If you recall there are four primary causes of IMS:

    1. Hormonal fluctuations.

    2. Changes in brain chemistry.

3. Increased stress.

4. Loss of male identity and purpose.

Whether a man is gay or straight, his hormone levels are going to decrease as he gets older. Gay or straight, his brain chemistry will change depending on his eating habits, exercise preferences, and general health. Gay or straight, he will be affected by stresses that impact his lives. Gay or straight, male identity and sense of purpose can erode over time and cause a man become more "testy," irritable, and angry.

So it's important for gay men to recognize that most of what I've been saying in this book will apply to them as well. Although it is primarily written for women (mostly because they are the ones who have been asking for such a book), it is really for anyone who is in a relationship with a man who may be going through IMS.

Having said that, however, there are some aspects of "gay irritable male syndrome" that are worth discussing in more depth. I can then suggest tools that you can use later to improve things with your partner. Let's start with some basics that may seem obvious, but can help us better deal with IMS.

1. Both halves of the partnership are male.

Regardless of sexual orientation, the fact that we grow up male creates some interesting dynamics. First, we all come out of the body of a woman, who is our first love object. As boys we have to separate from her and move towards a male father-figure to find our male identity. That's not easy for any males and has its unique nuances for gay men.

We all struggle with what it means to be a "boy." As boys begin to sense that they are different, there is often confusion about "who I am" and "am I normal." As we get older and begin to deal with sexual attractions, gay boys have to struggle to recognize, own, and accept their interest in other boys in a society that is still terribly homophobic.

2. Both of you have testosterone levels that likely vary.

It's been called the "hormone from hell" and "the fountain of youth." It is blamed for wars, gang violence, rape, and the body and mind of Sylvester Stallone. It is credited with making men strong, shrinking their bellies, protecting their heart, and boosting sexual desire in both men and women. It is perhaps the most misunderstood player in the human sexual symphony. It is what makes those born with an XY chromosome, male. It is testosterone. Here's how it works.

In the first weeks in the womb, the tiny fetus is neither male nor female. It has all the basic equipment to develop as either sex. At around six weeks, the sexual identity is finally determined when the special cells in the testes produce male hormones, the main one being testosterone. It helps craft the penis, the scrotum and testicles, along with the contouring of the body—very valuable additions if you are a male.

We don't get much action from this hormone until it is awakened with a bang when the boy reaches puberty, and testosterone levels rise 400-1000%. "Teenage boys become walking grenades, just waiting to go off," says Theresa Crenshaw, M.D., author of *The Alchemy of Love and Lust*, and an expert on hormonal changes in men and women. "As production kicks into high gear, the psychological and physical impact of testosterone is overwhelming. More than any other substance, testosterone controls the development and maintenance of masculine characteristics."

We all know that men have more testosterone than women, but few of us realize that there is a great deal of variation in the levels of testosterone between different males. We inherit our testosterone level, just as we inherit our height, body build, eye-color, cholesterol level, and other characteristics. Depending on these unique characteristics, our normal, healthy testosterone levels may range from 350 ng./dl to 1000 ng/dl of blood when we are young men.

Most guys have a tendency to think that more is better; the truth is that some of us are Low T type guys. Some of us are Middle T type guys. And some of us are High T. Like our height and body type we can seek to change them, but there are real limits, and accepting ourselves the way we are is part of becoming mature, healthy adults.

3. Sexuality as we age can be confusing.

Gay or straight, sexuality and aging can be difficult. We live in a youth-obsessed culture where the goal for many seems to be to stay forever young. We all get older and we all have to deal with age and infirmities in our own ways. Whatever our inherited level of hormones, they will decrease with age. Some men's testosterone levels drop more rapidly. For others it is a slower process of decline. Males, unlike females, have hormone levels that generally remain high enough to be able to make babies until later in life.

As a result, male sex drive, or at least the desire for younger more attractive partners, continues into old age. Whether gay or straight, whether we are wanting children or not, our higher testosterone levels keep "looking." This can be a source of joy or a source of conflict for men as they age. Women often fear that their man will leave for a younger woman. Many gay men have dual vulnerability. They have to worry that they might stray and also worry that their partner may become interested in someone else.

So what are things you can do if your partner is going through Irritable Male Syndrome?

1. Remember, "I'm not the target."

When our partner seems to be directing their anger our way, it's difficult not to feel that we are the target of their negative feelings. There is a tendency to feel "attacked." Our response is usually then to retreat or to attack back. Neither solution works very well. Fighting back just adds fuel to a fire that is already burning out of control. Retreating can leave the partner feeling afraid, ashamed, and confused. Often their anger and irritability is an expression of their pain and vulnerability. They need love and understanding, even though they act in ways that make you want to go into a "fight or flight" mode.

It helps if you can remember, "I'm not the target. My partner is upset and frustrated, but it is not my fault. The energy he's sending may be coming my way, but I'm not the target and I don't have to let his angry feelings hurt me. I can resist the temptation to let his unkind words or actions sink in. I can stay focused on the feelings he's expressing and see if I can figure out what he needs. Does he need care, understanding, solace, support?"

Let him know you want to understand what's going on and want to be as supportive as you can be. Let him know it isn't always easy to listen well when you become upset, angry, or scared; and tell him you're doing your best to take care of yourself and be there for him.

2. Take good care of yourself.

It isn't easy supporting someone who is acting angry and mean. Even though you may understand and empathize, it can still take its toll. IMS can go on for a long time, so you have to be willing to see this as a marathon. You'll need to be in good shape and keep taking good care of yourself along the way. Eat well, get plenty of rest, take physical exercise, and do relaxation exercises.

Remember, too, that you may have your own tendencies towards IMS. It might be good for both of you to take the quiz at *www.IMSquiz.com*. You can each score yourselves and then take the quiz as you see your partner's behavior. It's a good way to open communications and it can also help you monitor your progress.

3. Talk about past losses and humiliations.

Often IMS is triggered by losses in our lives. These could include loss of status at work, loss of income, job losses, the loss of our hair, of our stamina, the loss of our youthful appearance, of our health, the loss of our dreams. These losses, if unexpressed, can lead to IMS.

But we have also experienced more basic losses and humiliations in our earlier years. Recent losses can trigger these more primal losses from when we were ridiculed or abused as children, when our parents beat us or ignored us, when we were teased or threatened, when our burgeoning emotional and sexual life was forced to be hidden or distorted.

Talking about these issues, even those we thought we had worked through and no longer impact our lives, can be very healing. It helps us recognize that we are not alone, and reminds ourselves and our partners how vulnerable we still are. It can help us to be more compassionate with ourselves, with our partners, with our families, and with our friends.

Use this space to write down your own experiences. In what ways do you see IMS manifesting with yourself and/or your partner? What can you do to make things better? What are some of the losses and wounds you've experienced? How can you be supportive of each other in your healing journey?

NOTES

PART III:

Addressing the Cause

of the Problem

Chapter 16: What Is the Irritable Male Syndrome (IMS) and Why Is It So Dangerous?

Dear Dr. Diamond,

My fiancé recently broke off our engagement, of just short of a year, because she said I had changed. She stated that no matter what she said I would "bite her head off", that I was no longer showing her affection, that she felt she had to "walk on eggshells" around me, and that I became very distant and unemotional.

A random stranger overheard me talking to one of my friends about my situation and mentioned Irritable Male Syndrome, so I went to the bookstore and decided to purchase the book. I had never heard of IMS, but now a lot of what's been going on with me makes sense. I feel real hope now that I can repair the damage to our relationship. Thank you. JT.

THE IRRITABLE MALE SYNDROME STORY

In order to get a clear understanding of IMS, it helps to know the story. When writing my book, *Male Menopause,* I discovered just how significant hormonal changes were in the lives of these men. Though mid-life men are still reluctant to recognize how much they are influenced by hormonal shifts, women immediately "got it." "I *knew* there was something 'hormonal' about his behavior," many women told me in talking about their mates. "Now, a lot of his behavior makes sense."

Another thing that became evident was how similar mid-life male changes were to the changes that young men go through between the ages of 15 and 25 as they make the transition from childhood to adulthood. Both groups of males experienced significant hormonal changes. Both groups went through marked emotional ups and downs. Both were sorting out and dealing with developing a new identity. And both were dealing with significant sexual changes.

I saw how much stress these men were under, most of it beyond and outside their awareness. They expressed their stress in different ways: some drank, others became depressed; some became aggressive, others withdrew and hid; some had heart attacks, others had nervous breakdowns.

I found that men going through male menopause were expressing a constellation of feelings and behaviors that seemed to reflect different aspects and intensities of "irritability." These included such things as: hypersensitivity, impatience, anger, blame, defensiveness, arguing, sullenness, silence, and withdrawal. Further, these men went from being nice and considerate to being mean and destructive, seemingly overnight. They could also go back and forth between acting loving and hateful, time and time again.

In early 2002, a colleague sent me a copy of an article by Dr. Gerald A. Lincoln, a researcher in Edinburgh, Scotland. He titled the paper, *the irritable male syndrome*, and described what he observed in male animals following the withdrawal of testosterone. He found that when animals had *low* testosterone, they became irritable, and tried to bite researchers and other animals. After working with rams and reindeer, he speculated that "irritable male syndrome" may be a problem for all male mammals and wondered whether it might hold true for human beings as well.

Based on my research on male menopause, I thought humans were more complex than other mammals, but we might suffer from the same syndrome. I decided I needed to talk to Dr. Lincoln directly and review his research. My wife, Carlin, and I arranged the trip to Edinburgh and met Dr. Lincoln and his family. We visited his research facility, and watched the animals become edgy, ill-tempered, and irritable when their testosterone was lowered. I came away convinced that irritable male syndrome was real and needed to be studied in humans.

WHAT EXACTLY IS IRRITABLE MALE SYNDROME?

After studying IMS for nearly 10 year now, I have a pretty clear picture of what we are dealing with. Here's how I define Irritable Male Syndrome:

A state of hypersensitivity, anxiety, frustration, and anger that occurs in males and is associated with biochemical changes, hormonal fluctuations, stress, and loss of male identity.

The medical community is notoriously slow in recognizing new problems. However, a few pioneering practitioners are beginning to understand IMS. "IMS is incredibly common—up to 30 percent of men experience it," says Christopher Steidle, M.D., clinical associate professor of urology at the Indiana University School of Medicine. "This is a male version of PMS, or premenstrual syndrome."

In this chapter we'll examine the core symptoms of IMS. In the next chapter we'll look at the four key causes of IMS: biochemical changes in brain chemistry, hormonal fluctuations, stress, and loss of male identity. Working with men (and those who live with them) who are experiencing IMS, I have found there are four core symptoms that underlie many others: hypersensitivity, anxiety, frustration and anger.

1. Hypersensitivity.

The women who live with these men say things like the following:

- *I feel like I have to walk on eggshells when I'm around him.*
- *I never know when I'm going to say something that will set him off.*
- *He's like a time bomb ready to explode but I never know when.*
- *Nothing I do pleases him.*
- *Whenever I try to do nice things, he pushes me away.*
- *He'll change in an eye-blink. One minute he's warm and friendly. The next he's cold and mean.*

The men don't often recognize their own hypersensitivity. Rather, their perception is that they are fine but everyone else is going out of their way to irritate them. The guys say things like:

- *Quit bothering me.*
- *Leave me alone.*
- *No, nothing's wrong. I'm fine.*
- *The kids always....* (Fill in the blank). It's usually something negative.
- *You never....* (Fill in the blank) e.g. *want sex, do what I want to do, think before you open your mouth, do things the right way.*
- *You damn....* (Fill in the blank) e.g. *fool, bitch.* As IMS progresses the words get more hurtful.
- They don't say anything. They increasingly withdraw into a numbing silence.

One concept I have found helpful is the notion that many of us are "emotionally sunburned," but our partners don't know it. We might think of a man who is extremely sunburned and gets a loving hug from his wife. He cries out in anger and pain. He assumes she knows he's sunburned so if she "grabs" him she must be trying to hurt him. She has no idea he is sunburned and can't understand why he reacts angrily to her loving touch. You can see how this can lead a couple down a road of escalating confusion.

2. Anxiety.

Anxiety is a state of apprehension, uncertainty, and fear resulting from the anticipation of a realistic, or fantasized, threatening event or situation. IMS men live in constant worry and fear. There are many real threats that they are dealing with—sexual changes, job insecurities, relationship problems. There are also many uncertainties that lead men to ruminate and fantasize about future problems.

3. Frustration.

IMS men feel blocked in attaining what they want and need in life. They often don't even know what they need. When they do know, they may think there's no way they can get it. They often feel defeated in the things they try to do to improve their lives. These men feel frustrated in their relationships with family, friends, and at work. The world is changing and they don't know where, how, or if they fit in.

Author Susan Faludi captures this frustration in her book *Stiffed: The Betrayal of the American Man.* The frustration is expressed in the question that is at the center of her study of American males. "If, as men are so often told, they are the dominant sex, why do so many of them feel dominated, done in by the world?" This frustration, that is frequently hidden and unrecognized, is a key element of IMS.

4. Anger.

Anger can be simply defined as a strong feeling of displeasure or hostility. Yet anger is a complex emotion. Outwardly expressed it can lead to aggression and violence. When it is turned inward it can result in depression and suicide. Anger can be direct and obvious or it can be subtle and covert. Anger can be loud or quiet. It can be expressed as hateful words, hurtful actions, or in stony silence.

For many men, anger is the only emotion they have learned to express. Growing up male, we are taught to avoid anything that is seen as the least bit feminine. We are taught that men "do" while women "feel." As a result men learn to keep all emotions under wrap. We cannot show we are hurt, afraid, worried, or panicked. The only feeling that is sometimes allowed to many men is anger. When men begin going through IMS, it is often anger that is the primary emotion.

If these symptoms are not addressed adequately they tend to get worse. Over a period of weeks, months, and years, the pressure builds up. Often it explodes, seemingly out of the blue. One day he appears to be fine. The next, he's claiming he's had enough and he wants to leave. Most women I've talked with say they felt that something wasn't right, but they didn't have the understanding and the courage to deal with it directly. Don't let this happen to you.

Many women suffer indirectly from IMS as they see the man they love becoming more and more unhappy, angry, and withdrawn. They also suffer directly as they increasingly become the target of his angry and erratic moods. The relationship that they have lovingly built through the years begins to crumble. This is more than painful. It is a tragedy.

In this space write down the behaviors you are observing in the man in your life. In what ways is he hypersensitive, anxious, frustrated, and angry? How have his feelings impacted you?

NOTES

NOTES

Chapter 17: What Causes Irritable Male Syndrome?

Dear Dr. Jed,

Over the past three years especially, I have noticed that my rela-
tionship with my wife has begun to deteriorate. In the past there
were open displays of affection and frequent verbal affirmations.
Now, I seem to be irritable all the time. My attitude seems to be
"don't come near me, don't talk to me, I had a hard day, I want the
entire world to piss off."

She now rarely tries to hug me, never initiates sex, and talks to
me about half as much as she used to. It's gotten to the point where
I find out what's going on in her life from my mother or sisters.
We're both miserable and it's ruining our lives. I don't understand
what is causing me to act this way. Can you help me? Robert.

Based on research and feedback involving more than 60,000
men, we have a much better understanding of what is causing
IMS. In the previous chapter we discussed the primary symptoms
of IMS, here we discuss causes. Although triggers vary, man to
man, we found that there were four key elements at the core of
most men's problems: 1) Hormonal fluctuations, 2) Biochemical
changes in brain chemistry, 3) Increasing stress, 4) Loss of male
identity and purpose.

1. Hormones and IMS

In order to understand the way in which hormonal fluctuations
cause IMS in men, we need to know something about testosterone.
Theresa L. Crenshaw, M.D., author of *The Alchemy of Love and*
Lust, describes testosterone this way: "Testosterone is the young
Marlon Brando—sexual, sensual, alluring, dark, with a dangerous
undertone." She goes on to say that "It is also our 'warmone,'
triggering aggression, competitiveness, and even violence. *Testy* is
a fitting term." We know that men with testosterone levels that
are *too high* can become angry and aggressive. But recent research

shows that most hormonal problems in men are caused by testosterone levels that are *too low.*

Dr. Gerald Lincoln, who coined the term "Irritable Male Syndrome," found that lowering levels of testosterone in his research animals caused them to become more irritable, biting their cages as well as the researchers who were testing them. Larrian Gillespie, M.D., an expert on male and female hormones says, "Low testosterone is associated with symptoms of Irritable Male Syndrome."

2. Brain-Chemistry Changes and IMS

Most people have heard of the brain neurotransmitter, serotonin. When we have enough flowing through our brains, we feel good. When there isn't enough, we feel bad. Siegfried Meryn, M.D., author of *Men's Health and the Hormone Revolution* calls serotonin "the male hormone of bliss." Women have the same hormone in their brains and it has an equally positive effect on them. "The more serotonin the body produces," says Dr. Meryn, "the happier, more positive and more euphoric we are. Low serotonin can contribute to a man's irritability and aggression."

One of the most common causes of low serotonin levels is our eating and drinking habits. For instance, research has shown that protein, if consumed in excessive quantity, suppresses central nervous system serotonin levels. Many men were taught to believe that eating lots of meat would make them manly. Not only are there hormones injected in meat to make the animals fatter, but the protein contained in the meat can be harmful as well.

Judith Wurtman, Ph.D., and her colleagues at the Massachusetts Institute of Technology found that a high protein, low carbohydrate diet can cause increased irritability in men. They found that men often mistake their cravings for healthy carbohydrates, such as those found in vegetables like potatoes, rice, corn, squash, etc., with cravings for protein found in meat. "Eating protein when we need carbohydrates," says Wurtman, "will make us grumpy, irritable, or restless."

Wurtman's team also found that alcohol consumption increases serotonin levels initially. However, chronic use dramatically lowers serotonin, resulting in depression, carbohydrate cravings, sleep disturbances, and proneness to argumentativeness and irritability. It may be that the male propensity to eat too much meat and drink too much alcohol is contributing to lower serotonin levels in brain chemistry, which leads to symptoms of IMS.

3. Stress and IMS

We all know the feeling. We've had another one of those days at work. One deadline after another, and there isn't enough time to breathe. Someone is always making more demands, and no matter how hard we try to stay on top of things, we seem to be getting farther and farther behind. Many of us have lost our jobs. If we have a job, we're often working more hours for less money. The economy is in turmoil. Our savings are dwindling, and our hopes for retirement seem to be fading away. We all recognize the feeling of being *stressed out*. But what exactly is stress and why is stress-reduction so important?

In my experience as a psychotherapist, I have found that stress underlies most of the psychological, social, and medical problems that people face in contemporary society, including IMS. For most of us, stress is synonymous with worry. If it is something that makes us worry, then it is stressful.

We can't avoid stress, nor would we want to. Life is change and change is life. The problem arises when there is too much change in too short a time. We might think of the problem that leads to the Irritable Male Syndrome as "dis-stress" or "overstress." Stress is unavoidable, necessary, invigorating and life-enhancing. Distress and overstress can cause untold difficulties if not understood and prevented.

So, what can we do to relieve the build up of stress? There's actually a very simple answer. If you think about the kinds of stresses our bodies are designed to meet, they all involve physical activity. When a wild animal came into the camp of our hunter-gatherer ancestors, we either fought or ran away. In either case, we utilized a lot of physical energy. It's physical activity that allows the body to attend to the stress and then to return to normal.

In our modern world, we usually don't have wild animals bursting into our living rooms. The stresses are more psychological than physical. Yet the reaction is the same. Our bodies release stress hormones that can only be dissipated through physical activity. So, if you build up stress every day, you must do something physical every day. Walk, run, take an aerobics class. As the saying goes, "just do it." You'll feel better and it's a sure-fire way to treat IMS.

4. Loss of Male Identity and Purpose and IMS

For most of human history, the male role was clear. Our main job was to "bring home the bacon." We hunted for our food and shared what we killed with family and tribe. Everyone had a role to play. Some were good at tracking animals. Others excelled at making bows and arrows or spears. Some men were strong and could shoot an arrow with enough force to kill a buffalo. Others were skilled at singing songs and doing dances that invoked the spirit of the animal and made the hunt more effective.

But now many of us work at jobs that we hate, producing goods or services that have no real value to the community. We've gotten farther and farther away from the basics of bringing home food we've hunted or grown by ourselves. The money we receive is small compensation for doing work that is meaningless. And the men with some kind of job, no matter how bad, are the lucky ones. More and more men are losing their jobs and can't easily find new ones.

In her book, *Stiffed: The Betrayal of the American Man,* author Susan Faludi concludes that male stress, shame, depression, and violence are not just a problem of individual men, but a product of the social betrayal that men feel as a result of the changing economic situation we all face. One of the men Faludi talked to at length, Don Motta, could be speaking for millions of men in this country who have been laid off, been downsized, or part of a company that has gone under.

"There is no way you can feel like a man," says Motta. "You can't. It's the fact that I'm not capable of supporting my family... When you've been very successful in buying a house, a car, and could pay for your daughter to go to college, though she didn't want to, you have a sense of success and people see it. I haven't been able to support my daughter. I haven't been able to support my wife. I'll be very frank with you," he said slowly, placing every word down as if each were an increasingly heavy weight. "I. Feel. I've. Been. Castrated."

As Faludi interviewed men all across the country, she uncovered a fact that most men and women know all too well. Men put a lot of their identity and sense of self-worth into their jobs. If we aren't working or can't support our family, we feel that we're not really men. Motta's feeling of being castrated, speaks volumes. Even men who choose to retire, often feel lost and inadequate. We need to help men know that there is more to who they are than a paycheck. But we also have to develop societies that create meaningful work that can provide a decent living.

ALL FOUR ARE RELATED

Any one of the four causes mentioned above could have a major impact on a man and contribute to IMS. But what makes it even more difficult is that they interact with each other. When a man doesn't feel he has meaningful work, for instance, his stress levels go up and his testosterone levels go down. When men are stressed they often drink too much, which lowers their testosterone as well as their serotonin levels.

The good news is that by changing any one, we can impact all of them. Here are a few things a man can do now. Have his hormone levels checked. Find out if his testosterone is low. Eat healthy food with a balance of carbohydrates, fats, and proteins. Exercise every day. Look for work that is meaningful, and he should not take it personally if our dysfunctional economy pushes him out of his job. He should grow something he can eat, even it's just a carrot or potato.

In this space write down the ways in which your man's hormonal fluctuations, biochemical changes, increasing stress, and loss of male identity and purpose may be impacting you. How are they impacting the man in your life? Resist the temptation to immediately go and tell him what to do. Rather, listen deeply. Put yourself in his shoes. Get in touch with his feelings and his needs. It takes time to deal with these issues. Be patient. Be kind.

NOTES

NOTES

Chapter 18: How Do I Know If He Has IMS?

Dear Dr. Diamond,

I am a 45-year-old male experiencing a divorce which was initiated by my wife the day after Thanksgiving. I first became aware of your book while looking in the self help section of my bookstore last fall. I then decided to get on the website and check things out. I took the quiz and scored 102. However I did not seek help at that time.

I thought that I could handle things on my own and felt that my wife was the cause of my unhappiness. I now realize that was a big mistake. I know that if I sought help for my depression, I would have been able to see my relationships in a more realistic manner and that I would probably still be in my house with my loved ones enjoying the holidays instead of being kicked out and on my own.

Unfortunately for me the damage has been done and I realize that it is probably too late for me to reconcile with my wife. I now understand that IMS is a devastating condition and that depression can ruin lives as well as kill people. Thank you for your dedication to raising awareness of the devastating effects of depression, the irritable male syndrome, and male menopause.

I hope more people take the IMS quiz and act on what they learn, not wait too long like I did. Ted.

When I first began seeing men who I felt were having a problem with IMS, I just used my intuition and clinical experience to assess how serious the problem was and how best to treat it. I knew I needed an evaluation questionnaire that would be more specific and accurate. I developed a quiz and posted it on-line. I didn't know whether anyone would use it. To my surprise, within a few weeks 6,000 men, including Ted, had taken the quiz.

Since the quiz was first posted, 60,000 men and women from all over the world have taken it. Men take the quiz to better understand themselves. Women take it to better understand the man in their lives. We've learned a great deal about men including the following:

- Stress is a significant issue for men.

Only 8% say they are never stressed. 46% say they are often or almost always stressed.

- Sex is a major concern.

40% of the men say they are rarely or never sexually satisfied.

- Depression and Irritability are related.

21% of the men say they are depressed often or almost always. Only 9% say they are almost never irritable. 40% are irritable often or almost always.

- Men want to escape.

Only 7% say they almost never have a desire to *"get away* from *it all."* A surprising 62% say they often or almost always desire to escape.

TAKE THE IMS QUIZ

I ask the men completing the questionnaire to look as deeply and honestly as they can at feelings and actions that may be difficult to acknowledge. For women, I ask you also to be honest about how you see the man. Some of you may have a tendency to deny how violent things have become. Others of you may have difficulty recognizing and accepting how much pain your man is experiencing.

In the last month, reflect on how often you believe the man in your life has experienced the following feelings:

	NOT AT ALL	SOMETIMES	FREQUENTLY	MOST OF THE TIME
	0	**1**	**2**	**3**
1. Angry				
2. Impatient				
3. Blaming				
4. Dissatisfied				
5. Moody				
6. Fearful				
7. Discontented				
8. Hypersensitive				
9. Exhausted				
10. Grumpy				
11. Easily Upset				
12. Bored				
13. Aggressive				
14. Unloved				
15. Unappreciated				
16. Tense				
17. Touchy				
TOTAL				

	NOT AT ALL	SOMETIMES	FREQUENTLY	MOST OF THE TIME
	0	**1**	**2**	**3**
18. Tired				
19. Unloving				
20. Lonely				
21. Hostile				
22. Overwhelmed				
23. Destructive				
24. Demanding				
25. Depressed				
26. Frustrated				
27. Withdrawn				
28. Mean				
29. Sad				
30. Scared				
31. Numb				
32. Explosive				
33. Defensive				
34. Denies problems				
35. Critical				
TOTAL				

	NOT AT ALL	SOMETIMES	FREQUENTLY	MOST OF THE TIME
	0	**1**	**2**	**3**
36. Troubled				
37. A desire to over-eat				
38. A desire to drink or use drugs				
39. A need to withdraw behind T.V. Newspapers, or Computer				
40. A desire for increased time at work				
41. A need to sleep more or have trouble with sleep				
42. Impulsive				
43. Worried				
44. Lack of intimacy				
45. A pull to argue and fight				
46. Sarcastic				
47. Jealous				
TOTAL				

	NOT AT ALL	SOMETIMES	FREQUENTLY	MOST OF THE TIME
	0	**1**	**2**	**3**
48. Stressed				
49. Uncom- passionate				
50. Uncom- municative				
TOTAL				

It's not always easy to know how someone is feeling, but do your best. For each feeling listed, check whether it is true of you (or the person you are rating) not at all or rarely (score 0), sometime (score 1), frequently (score 2), or most of the time (score 3). Thus the final score can range from 0 to 150.

Based on my clinical experience and work with thousands of men, and the women who love them, we interpret the scores as follows:

- 0-25: None or few signs of IMS.
- 26-49: Some indications of IMS. May need help or watchful waiting to see if things improve or get worse.
- 50-75: IMS is likely and it is advisable to seek help.
- 76 and higher: IMS is definitely present and getting help is most important.

You can also take the quiz on-line at *www.IMSquiz.com*. Many women take the quiz and mark scores, as *they see* the man in their lives. They then ask the man to take the quiz and see what his score is. Often men are surprised at how high they are scoring.

Here's a place for you to write your thoughts. In reflecting on the man in your life, what was his IMS score? How does that fit with what you have experienced being with him? Which items cause you the most distress? Write down other feelings or behaviors that have been causing problems.

Notes

Chapter 19: What Are the 7 Most Common Types of IMS and How Do I Know Which Kind My Man Has?

Dear Dr. Diamond,

I want to thank you for your informative website. I believe my husband has these conditions you speak about. We have been married for 27 years and I began to notice these symptoms after our first child was born in 1985. It has continued to get worse. In the last few years I can hardly stand to be around him. Fortunately, he travels very often with work.

When he is not traveling, our home environment is tense and touchy, with people walking on eggshells all the time. When he is away, it is like a completely different home – so relaxed and people are at ease. I understand there are different types of IMS. Can you help me figure out which type my husband has? LM

When we first began testing people to see whether they had IMS and how serious it was, we gave them the IMS quiz and scored their results (See chapter 18). As more and more people from all over the world took the quiz, we found that their answers tended to group together and they exhibited seven different types of IMS. You can learn which type of IMS your man may be experiencing by reviewing the symptoms associated with each type:

TYPE 1: GRUMPY

Men who fall into this type are often hypersensitive. Little things can set them off and they easily become annoyed and angry. They are sure that someone else (usually their partner, family, or co-workers) is doing things to irritate them. It's the people who live with them who generally bear the brunt of it. This is the most common type, and the most difficult for the men to recognize. The following items from the quiz are associated with this type: Angry (1), Impatient (2), Blaming (3), Moody (5), Grumpy (10), Easily Upset (11), and Depressed (25).

TYPE 2: FEARFUL

Men who fall into this category tend to be fearful and worried. They feel that if something can go wrong, it probably will. They are often frustrated, but won't admit it. They may mope about and appear sad, but when pressed they can become sarcastic and mean. When you withdraw, they feel threatened and can become "clingy" and demanding. The following items from the quiz are associated with this type: Fearful (6), Frustrated (26), Mean (28), Sad (29), Denies problems (34), Worried (43), and Sarcastic (46).

TYPE 3: AGGRESSIVE

Men who fall into this category are very angry. They can be hostile and aggressive one minute, then withdraw into silence the next. Minor disturbances may flare up into full-blown fights. They might seem serene and quiet on the surface, but when they feel threatened, they can go into attack mode. They may break things in anger, hit the wall, and at times become physically abusive. On the highway, they can become the poster boys for road rage. The following items from the quiz are associated with this type: Angry (1), Aggressive (13), Hostile (21), Destructive (23), Demanding (24), Withdrawn (27), and Numb (31).

TYPE 4: UNLOVED

Men who fall into this category often feel unappreciated and unloved. You can praise them over and over, but inside they feel empty. No matter how much reassurance you give, it never seems to be enough. They have great difficulty expressing deep feelings of love and affection. Like many of the types, they often suffer from childhood abuse and/or abandonment, particularly if the scores are high. They hunger for love and support, but often push people away with their sharp words. The following items from the quiz are associated with this type: Discontented (7), Unloved (14), Unappreciated (15), Unloving (19), Lonely (20), Frustrated (26), and Sarcastic (46).

TYPE 5: JEALOUS

Men who fall into this category are insecure and can easily become jealous. They are possessive and will react with hostility if they aren't getting enough of your attention. They are easily threatened and may become frustrated when they confront even small obstacles. They are often fearful and defensive, but resort to aggression when stressed. These men may appear quite independent and self-sufficient, yet, underneath their bravado, they are often frightened of being alone. The following items from the quiz are associated with this type: Unloving (19), Frustrated (26), Scared (30), Defensive (33), Withdraws to T.V., computer, or newspaper (39), Jealous (47), and Stressed (48).

TYPE 6: EXHAUSTED

Men who fall into this category are tired a good deal of the time. They feel stressed at home and at work. Life can seem overwhelming and they may entertain fantasies of escape. Their energy level is low and they seem to be "running on empty." They may have difficulty sleeping. Often, they feel they haven't lived up to their potential. The following items from the quiz are associated with this type: Exhausted (9), Tense (16), Tired (18), Overwhelmed (22), Withdraws to T.V., computer, or newspaper (39), Spends increased time at work (40), and Sleep problems (41).

TYPE 7: IMPULSIVE

Men who fall into this category are unpredictable. They can be excitable and explosive. When they are feeling at their best they may seem lively, fun, and the life of the party. But their "dark side" can be dangerous. They may have rigid expectations, and be very demanding. When they are down, they can become defensive and argumentative. Things will be going along well and all of a sudden something sets them off and they blow up. The following items from the quiz are associated with this type:

Demanding (24), Explosive (32), Desire to drink or use drugs (38), Impulsive (42), Lack of intimacy (44), Tendency to argue and fight (45), and Sarcastic (46).

IMS men will usually exhibit some symptoms in all the types. However, if you look at the scores for these symptoms, you'll find that there are one or two types (sometimes more) where the scores are higher than the others. For instance, you may find your man scores highest on Type 1, "Grumpy", but also scores high on Type 2, "Fearful."

Knowing which types predominate for your man can help you better tune into his feelings and concerns. It can also help to prepare yourself so that you aren't blind-sided by his emotional ups and downs. Most women are surprised at their man's change of behavior and seem baffled by his feelings. Having a better understanding of what is going on will help you protect yourself while you're supporting him.

Write down your thoughts here. Which type(s) of IMS is affecting your man the most? How does it impact you? Write down the symptoms associated with the type(s) that your man experiences the most. Which of the symptoms cause you the greatest problems?

NOTES

Chapter 20: My Man is Irritable and Very Unhappy. Could He Be Depressed?

Dear Dr. Diamond,

I knew there was something wrong when I met him at the airport after he returned from seeing his family. He was very moody, said nothing was wrong, but clearly something was going on with him. When we made love, he found it difficult to obtain an erection, but got angry when I tried to talk with him about it. Things have continued to get worse over the last few months. He seems terribly unhappy, agitated, angry, and blaming. My sister has suffered from depression and she was sad, tearful, and didn't have any energy. He acts very different, but I wonder if he could be depressed. Jl.

"Sadness isn't macho—this Eric Weaver knew," wrote Susan Freinkel, in an article titled *The Secret Men Won't Admit* in the January 2007 issue of *Reader's Digest*. "When depression engulfed the Rochester, New York, police sergeant, it took a different guise: anger. To the former SWAT team leader and competitive body-builder, it was manly, and easy, to be mad."

The father of three, then in his early 30s, stewed in a near-constant state of anger, the story reported. "One minute I'd be okay and the next minute I'd be screaming at my kids and punching the wall," he recalls. "My kids would ask, 'What's wrong with Daddy? Why's he so mad all the time?' I probably heard that 1,000 times." For years, Weaver didn't know what was wrong. "I just thought I was a jerk." The possibility that he was depressed never occurred to him until the angry facade began to crumble, leaving him with no feelings except utter despair. The tears finally came one night when he admitted to his wife the painful truth: "I've thought about committing suicide every day."

Weaver's confusion about what afflicted him is not unusual. Though millions of men suffer from depression, many don't recognize the symptoms or seek help. "Men don't find it easy to ask for help," says Thomas Insel, MD, director of the *National Institute of Mental Health (NIMH)*. "That's a gene that must be on the Y chromosome."

Research I conducted on gender and depression, and reported in my book, *Male vs. Female Depression: Why Men Act Out and Women Act In,* convinces me that men often experience depression quite differently than do women. Women tend to "act in" their pain, and focus on internal judgments of their own inadequacies. Men, on the other hand, are conditioned to "act out" and thus men's depression is more likely to be expressed through chronic anger, self-destructiveness, drug use, gambling, womanizing and workaholism. Underlying these behaviors are experiences of loss, and persistent feelings of hopelessness, helplessness, and worth-lessness, the hallmarks of depression.

How can you tell if the man in your life is depressed? Here are symptoms that are often indicative of depression in males:

1. He feels that things are stacked against him.
2. He seems emotionally numb and closed down.
3. He feels sorry for himself and blames others for his problems.
4. He has trouble controlling his temper.
5. He is easily annoyed, becomes grumpy, or impatient.
6. When others disagree with him, he gets upset.
7. He uses drink, drugs, or sex as an escape.
8. He seems gloomy, negative, or hopeless.
9. He appears hostile even though he doesn't always let it show.
10. He has very little emotional energy.

I've found that answering "yes" to 5 or more of these symptoms is a positive sign of depression. It can be helpful to talk to a therapist who is trained to understand, diagnose, and treat depression in men. However, men are often in denial about their condition and refuse to get help. Some of them feel that seeing a counselor means they are "mentally ill" or that they need to be on medication.

Though medication can be helpful for some men, new research shows that a number of non-drug alternatives can be quite successful. And these are things that many men are willing to try. In his book, *The Depression Cure*, Stephen Ilardi, associate professor of clinical psychology, said the most effective way to cure depression was to make just a few simple changes to daily lifestyles and habits. These are similar to changes I recommend for my male clients.

Ilardi calls his program TLC, or Therapeutic Lifestyle Change, and offers 6 lifestyle elements that are based on the practices that were part of human life before we became so urbanized, stressed, and depressed. These include the following:

1. Exercise.

Three times a week get 35 minutes of aerobic exercise. Aerobic exercise is anything like running, walking fast, biking, or playing basketball, that gets your heart rate elevated to about 120-160 beats per minute. Anaerobic exercise (like yoga or weightlifting) is better than nothing, but the strongest antidepressant effects have been observed from aerobic exercise. Lots of people report that finding a regular exercise partner and routine helps them stay motivated.

2. Omega-3 fatty acid supplements.

You can buy these at a drugstore or health food store. Look for a brand that will give you 1000 mg of EPA and 500 mg of DHA per day. This is the amount that has been shown in studies to be beneficial to people with depression.

You can take these even if you are on antidepressant medication; there are no known interactions with drugs. The only side effects patients reported are that they sometimes burp up a fishy taste after taking them. A solution to this problem is to freeze the pills and take them right before a meal. If all else fails, there is a liquid form available that some people prefer.

3. Light exposure.

This element is most helpful to people who notice that there is a seasonal component to their depression. We recommend that people get at least 30 minutes of bright light exposure per day. You can actually go outside in the sun (take off the sunglasses, but leave on the sunscreen!) or get light exposure from a special light box that emits the same amount of light (10,000 lux).

You should try to get light exposure at the same time every day. Some people like to sit by the light box while they eat breakfast and read the paper. Some prefer to sit by it while they read a book or study during the evening. You may wish to experiment to see what seems best for you. And don't miss a day of light exposure if you can help it. This is something that will only work for you, cumulatively, if you are consistent.

4. Anti-rumination strategies.

Rumination is the habit that many depressed people get into, of dwelling on their negative thoughts. Rather than coming up with a solution to a problem and acting on it, people with depression often let their negative thoughts spiral out of control. It is important to recognize rumination for what it is and put a stop to it immediately. Rumination only makes people's moods worse. When you find yourself doing it, try one of these things: call a friend, exercise, write down the negative thoughts in a journal, or do some other pleasant activity (like walking or reading).

5. Social support.

You have probably noticed that as the man becomes more depressed, he is less motivated to seek out others for socializing. You can encourage him to spend as much time as possible with others. This is a powerful way to distract him from rumination and get him the support he needs.

I've found that family and friends can ask the man to help with some project that requires doing. Men will often respond to assist someone else, even when they don't have the energy to help themselves. Even a little bit of social interaction can break the negative cycle of anger, frustration, withdrawal, and more anger, frustration, and withdrawal.

6. Sleep hygiene.

Most of us need 8 hours of sleep per night and most of us are sleep deprived. Men generally get less sleep than women and for depressed men, lack of sleep can be debilitating. One of the biggest risk factors for depression is sleep deprivation.

It may take awhile to re-establish healthy sleeping habits. We often get used to sleeping less, and come to believe that we don't really need that much sleep. Here's what can help. Go to sleep at the same time every night. Prepare yourself for bed by having a "bedtime ritual". Dim the lights, turn off the TV and computer, put on your PJs, and do a quiet activity like reading. Avoid caffeine and alcohol for several hours before you plan to go to bed. A soothing back or foot rub before going to sleep can be a welcome relaxant.

It isn't easy living with a depressed person. You have to go out of your way to get the care and support you need, particularly when he isn't able to give it. Many people living with a depressed person can become depressed themselves. The steps listed above can be useful for you too.

Here's a place to write your thoughts. Which symptoms of depression does your man exhibit? Which ones are the most difficult for you to deal with? Which of the 6 health-enhancing elements does your man use now? Which ones would he be most willing to engage in? Remember, depression can be a serious problem, but it can be treated.

NOTES

Chapter 21: What Are the 8 Hidden Stressors That Are Causing IMS to Increase World-wide?

Dear Dr. Jed,

After reading about IMS on your website, I'm convinced that my husband is experiencing it and it's having a negative impact on our lives. He is forty-seven, soon to be forty-eight, and there have been some big changes in our lives. He quit smoking this past December, but long before that, his level of patience began to diminish noticeably. He has become very hard to live with. He becomes enraged so easily lately.

Whenever there is something around the house that requires his attention, he seems to get angry at me for bringing it up. But if I do something that he sees as "his job" like fixing the sink, he suddenly jumps down my throat. I end up walking on egg shells. I never know what will set him off.

We both travel a great deal for our jobs and meet a lot of people in other countries. It seems to be that IMS is happening everywhere. What's going on? Are people more stressed about things like work and relationship, or are there new stresses that we have to deal with? DT.

We live in a stressful time and it impacts men and women alike. Most everyone has heard of stress and most of us feel the stress of our lives, but not everyone really understands stress or how to deal with it.

Which of these is stress?

- You receive a promotion at work.
- Your car has a flat tire.
- You go to a fun party that lasts till 2:00 a.m.
- You have a fight with your spouse.
- Your new bedroom set is being delivered.
- You are worried about your relationship.
- You get a bad case of hay fever.
- All of the above.

All of these are stress.

If you are used to thinking that stress is something that makes you worry, you have the wrong idea of stress. Stress is many different kinds of things: happy things, sad things, allergic things, physical things. Many people carry enormous stress loads and they do not even realize it.

WHAT IS STRESS?

We are all familiar with the word "stress." Stress is when you are worried about getting laid off your job, or worried about having enough money to pay your bills, or worried about your spouse's health. In fact, to most of us, stress is synonymous with worry. If it is something that makes you worry, then it is stress.

Your body, however, has a much broader definition of stress. To your body, stress is synonymous with change. Anything that causes a change in your life causes stress. It doesn't matter if it is a "good" change, or a "bad" change, they are both stress. When your son gets married to a wonderful girl, that is stress. If you break your leg, that is stress. Good or bad, if it is a *change* in your life, it is stress as far as your body is concerned.

The reason mid-life is so stressful is because there are so many changes involved. Hormone levels are dropping, brain chemistry is changing, we put on weight, we lose strength and muscle mass, we worry about our health, the health of our parents, and the health of our children, our status at work is changing, our savings are often diminishing, and so on.

Even *imagined change* is stress. (Imagining change is what we call "worrying".) If you fear that you will not have enough money to pay your rent, that is stress. If you worry that you may get fired, that is stress. If you think that you may receive a promotion at work, that is also stress (even though this would be a good change). Whether the event is good or bad, imagining changes in your life is stressful.

HOLMES-RAHE STRESS TEST

We can't eliminate stress any more than we can stop our lives from changing. But too much stress can cause problems. How much is too much? Fortunately, there is an answer.

A number of years ago two doctors, Thomas Holmes and Richard Rahe, conducted a large research project which showed that the higher the stress score an individual had, the more likely it was they would get sick. For each life event they assigned a score based on how stressful the change was. For instance the death of a spouse was 100, divorce was 73, marital separation, 65, jail term 63, death of a close family member 63, personal injury or illness 53, marriage 50, fired at work 47, marital reconciliation 45, and so on.

If you score below 150, you have a 35% chance of illness or accident within 2 years, between 150-300, a 51% chance, and over 300, you have an 80% chance of illness or accident. Obviously this is a general measure. A divorce may be the most stressful change in their life for one person, but less so for another. Getting fired at work may be devastating to one person, but a relief to another. All will still be stressful, but the impact will vary.

MODERN STRESSES THAT WE MAY NOT REALIZE AFFECT US

We often think of stress as being "up-close" and personal. Things like a death in the family, divorce, or loss of income are clearly stressful. But we are often not aware of the impact of global stressors. We usually don't think of worldwide population increase, for instance, as a stress in our lives. However, at the present time we are adding 222,239 extra people to the planet *every day*. Those people impact us in direct and indirect ways, and contribute to the increased irritability and anger that we feel.

Here are eight worldwide stressors that are impacting our lives:
1. Economic implosion.
2. Environmental destruction.
3. The end of cheap oil.
4. Global warming.
5. Population overshoot.
6. Food practices that are killing us.
7. Male despair and global violence.
8. "Wild-card" event such as terrorist attack, environmental catastrophe, or flu pandemic.

As we take a brief look at each of these "hidden" stressors, think about how they may be impacting you and the man in your life.

1. Economic implosion.

Most of us are affected by various levels of economic collapse. It seems to me that our whole economic system is based on *growth*. We need to be creating more and more wealth to pay the interest on our increasing levels of debt. But we live on a finite planet, with limited resources. We cannot keep going on as we have. I believe we are all feeling the stress of our economic system collapsing.

2. Environmental destruction.

Usually we're not aware of the extent of the destruction until there's a big story in the news or we are touched personally. I recently visited the neighborhood where I grew up. I remembered lots of greenery, open space, and waterways. Now it's all been paved. We may not always see the extent of the destruction, but we feel it and it stresses us all.

3. The end of cheap oil.

Our whole system has been based on the supply of readily available and inexpensive fossil fuels. But this era is coming to an end. As much as we talk about and hope for "alternative energy," there really is nothing that can easily replace oil. We see these changes with the increasing costs of everything from gasoline to food. These stresses are bound to increase.

4. Global warming.

Although some people still believe it is a myth, almost all reputable scientists in the world recognize that we are heating up the planet and causing major changes. We are melting the icecaps, altering the weather, and upsetting the balance of nature. At present the carbon dioxide content of the atmosphere is 390 parts per million. Scientists tell us that we must reduce that below 350 or bring about massive destruction. That's a lot of change coming our way whether we act wisely or stay in denial.

5. Population overshoot.

We all know that the population of the world is increasing, and that puts stress on everything—land, water, air, and food. World Population Day is an annual event, which began on July 11, 1987. The day seeks to raise awareness about the ever-increasing population of the world. Think back to the world in 1987. On July 11,

1987 the estimated population of the world was 5 billion. In 2000, world population reached 6.06 billion. And by May 9, 2010 the world population was just over 6.8 billion (and counting) which indicates a 78 million increase in the population per year. It is feared that world population might reach up to 10.7 billion in the year 2050. Where are we planning to house all those people? How are we planning to feed them? Do you feel some of the stress?

6. Food practices that are killing us.

For the first time in human history there are more overweight people in the world (1.4 billion of us) than those who are starving (0.8 billion). The same corporate food policies that fatten us up on high calorie foods (and beverages) also keep people from growing their own food or being able to make a decent living to buy adequate food. We all feel the stress around our waists.

7. Male despair and global violence.

Comedian Elayne Boosler offered this comment: "When women are depressed they either eat or go shopping. Men invade another country." I believe there is some truth to that. It's also true that when men are depressed they often kill themselves. We all feel the stress of male despair turned outward in the form of violence and inward in the high rate of suicide in men vs. women.

8. "Wild-card" events such as terrorist attack or flu pandemic.

"Wild-cards" are events that we can't predict specifically (unlike things such as our current birth and death rate, and that population size will increase), but we know one or more of theses "wild-cards" will happen sometime. There may not ever be another terrorist attack, or the kind of flu pandemic that killed 100,000,000 people worldwide between 1918 and 1920, or the kind of devastating earthquake that struck Haiti. But they could happen and most of us worry about them.

So, what are we to do? There's a slogan we've all heard, "think globally and act locally." I'd suggest another one, "think about the future, but act in the present." We have to have our eyes open to the real changes we are facing. Putting our heads in the sand and pretending they don't exist won't lower our stress levels. But we can act in the present to deal more effectively with those things we can change.

All the imagined stress, all the worry, is about the future. Here's a simple cure for that kind of stress. Ask yourself the following question: "How are things right now?" 95% of the time, your answer will be "fine." When you say, "Yes, but what if..." you're creating stress about an imagined future. The truth is that most of what we worry about never happens.

If you're concerned about global warming, peak oil, our economic situation—and God knows I am—you need to take some action to make things better. I recommend you read *WorldShift, 2012: Making Green Business, New Politics & Higher Consciousness Work Together* by Ervin Laszlo and check out his website at *www.worldshift2012.org*. Don't worry about the future. Do what you can now, and let the future take care of itself.

Here's the place where you can write your thoughts. Have you had a lot of change in your life in the last year? If you had to rate the 8 modern stressors I mention, what score would you give each one? Does it feel as stressful as a spouse dying (100) or more like a vacation (13) or somewhere in between? If you're worrying about one, focus on it and take some constructive action. Join an organization dedicated to stopping global warming, such as www.350.org, for instance. Stressing ourselves doesn't help anyone, but peaceful, joyful, constructive action (particularly with other people you enjoy) can help a lot.

NOTES

NOTES

PART IV:

Getting Help

for Him and for You

Chapter 22: How Do I Help Him When He Refuses to Talk?

Dear Dr. Jed,

My boyfriend and I have been together for just over four years and I'm noticing terrible mood shifts that are increasingly difficult to live with. He becomes extremely frustrated, irritable, angry, confused, unsure, lost, and sad. I can tell that he is becoming more distant and I'm worried he's thinking of leaving.

Whenever I try and get him to talk about his unhappiness or what I can do to make things better, it seems to make him angry and he pulls away even more. I love him very much and I really think he loves me, but I feel our relationship slipping away and I don't know what to do. Please, can you help? BL

For men the 5 most dreadful words in the English language are, "Honey, we need to talk." The words can be said with anger or with love, with disdain or compassion, with despair or with hope. It seems no matter how they are presented, they are met with a resistance bordering on terror by most men. Why should a woman's desire to talk be met with such resistance?

"I feel caught in a horrible trap," one woman told me. "If I let things alone and don't say anything, our relationship continues to go downhill. If I try and talk to him about ways we can fix things, he acts like I'm trying to kill him. He refuses to talk and our relationship continues to deteriorate. What do I do to save us?"

FEAR AND SHAME FEEL LIKE LIFE AND DEATH FOR WOMEN AND MEN IN TROUBLE

In order to break through the impasse of how to help a man who refuses to talk about what is going on, we have to understand fear in women, shame in men, and how they interact with each other. Here's an experience many people have had which can serve to introduce us to this critically important topic. A man and his wife are in the car together on their way to visit family for the holidays. As he drives around a curve, the wife suddenly puts her hand on the dashboard to brace herself. He gives her a hostile look, clenches his jaw, and turns back to the road. Within minutes they get into a fight about some inconsequential issue that neither can remember. What happened?

Both are a bit on edge as the drive begins since it is holiday time and they are visiting family. When the man drives through the curve, the wheels hit the divider bumps briefly, the woman is startled, and she feels a jolt of *fear*. She braces herself—a reflexive attempt to protect herself. The man does not realize she is afraid. Instead, he interprets her reaction as a judgment on his driving and his ability to protect her from harm. He has a jolt of *shame*. In an attempt to protect himself from feeling inadequate he gets angry. His anger triggers more fear in his wife, which triggers more shame in him.

Further, he is not only ashamed, but he is ashamed of being ashamed. As a result he blocks the shame from his awareness and focuses instead on something he imagines his wife did to him. His wife may deny her own fear, thinking, "He's really a good driver, I don't have to worry." All of this goes on in a matter of seconds and is out of the awareness of both partners. But the result is that both act as though they were engaged in a life or death struggle over something that is so inconsequential they can't believe it is causing them to "lose it" with each other.

In order to understand the irritable male syndrome (and a whole lot of other problems that impact men and women) it's important to recognize the way in which talking about a problem can increase fear and shame for women and men.

THE EVOLUTION OF WOMEN'S FEAR

Our emotions are critical to our survival and have evolved over millions of years to keep us alive long enough to mate, raise children, and pass on our genes to the next generation. From an evolutionary perspective, women are the more valuable for the survival of the species. The woman carries the rare egg (each woman makes only 400 in her lifetime) in her body. Conception occurs in her womb, a baby grows within, is nurtured by her breast milk after birth, and is kept alive and raised by her until the child is ready to leave home. The man carries a huge number of tiny sperm (each man makes 500,000,000 sperm per day).

Compared to the woman's contribution, males have little to do with the actual business of reproduction, beyond producing sperm packaged in seminal fluid. Having a man around to help rear the children is very valuable, but as many women have learned, it isn't absolutely essential.

A female's primary need is to be *cherished*. From the moment of birth until the day she dies, she needs to feel that a "special someone" will protect and care for her and no other. Whenever this connection is threatened she feels *anxiety* and *fear*. "Over the millennia, females developed a kind of internal GPS that keeps them aware of closeness and distance in all their relationships," say Patricia Love and Steven Stosny, authors of *How to Improve Your Marriage Without Talking About It*. "When a woman feels close she can relax; when she feels distant, she gets anxious."

When there is a break in the connection with her man, a woman has to work hard to get the emotional nurturance she needs. You may need to reach out to other women or learn to love yourself more fully. Self-love is not incompatible with loving your man.

MALE SHAME: THE HIDDEN DRAGON THAT CAN KILL

In order to understand male shame, we have to understand men's basic insecurity. Let's start with the essence of maleness and look more closely at the sperm. Although the human egg is microscopic, it is large enough to house 250,000 sperm. Eggs weigh 85,000 times as much as sperm. Think how you'd feel if you had to merge with someone who was 85,000 times heavier than you? Now, think of the competition involved in mating. There are fifty million to five hundred million sperm per ejaculation. How would you feel competing against those numbers for the prized egg?

Since it is the female who carries the egg, males are the ones who have to compete with each other in order to be chosen by the female. Sexual competition is a replay of fertilization itself. Numerous males, like small, hyperactive sperm, compete among themselves for access to females.

Males often remember, with a great deal of shame, walking across a room and asking the "cute" girl to dance, only to be turned down and having to walk back to his seat feeling that all eyes are on him and people are saying to themselves, "loser, loser,

loser." This is the essence of male shame. We are always in competition with other males to be chosen by a female who can trigger our feelings of insufficiency and inadequacy with a casual shake of her head. And our shame deepens as others witness our retreat.

Women experience shame from the other side. She must sit and wait for a man to approach her. If she is assertive, she runs the risk of being shamed for being "pushy" and "unfeminine." She is judged, most often, on her looks and rejected if she doesn't meet the current standards of female beauty.

Men's basic need is for *respect*, just as women's basic need is to be *cherished*. He needs to feel like a winner, that he can beat the competition and be the chosen one. From the time he is born until the day he dies, he is vulnerable to shame and loss of face. The shame that men experience is a kind of soul murder, undermining the foundations of our masculine selves.

WHY TALKING CAN TRIGGER MEN'S SHAME AND WHAT WOMEN CAN DO INSTEAD

For most women, talking is the way they connect. It's how they deal with their fears and how they solve problems. When they see the man in their life suffering from the irritable male syndrome, they want to get him to talk about it in the hopes that they can help him heal.

But as noted at the beginning of the chapter, for men, talking often triggers shame. Here's why. The truth is that men talk all the time (though not as much as women) about many things. If you look back, he probably talked more when you were first getting together when he felt safe and his self-respect was high. But as relationships become threatened by IMS, the shame/fear dance takes over. Usually when women approach men for one of those "let's talk" moments, it's when she is afraid. This triggers his shame and he usually thinks, "What have I done wrong now?" As we have more and more of these encounters, the woman builds up more fear and the man builds up more shame until talking is the last thing he wants to do.

So how do you help him without talking?

1. Lower your fear levels.

It may not be evident at the moment, but one of man's strongest desires is to *protect* and *serve* the person he loves. When you're afraid, he judges himself as a poor protector. His shame levels goes up and he usually gets more irritable and angry. One of the best ways to lower your fear levels is to remind yourself that there is much that you can do to save a shaky relationship, even when he refuses to talk about it. Most women are afraid that if they can't get the man to change, all is lost. Throughout this book you will learn many things you can do to save yourself and rescue your relationship.

2. Quit demeaning your man.

Most women have no intention of shaming or demeaning their man, but as I noted earlier, it often occurs as women become more anxious, frightened, and insecure. To demean means to lower in dignity, honor, or standing. Just as men are surprised at the things that cause women to be afraid, women are often surprised at the things that increase men's shame. Here are a few ways that psychologist Pat Love noticed she had shamed the man in her life: excluding him from important decisions, robbing him of the opportunity to help, correcting what he said, questioning his judgment, giving unsolicited advice, overreacting, ignoring his needs, withholding praise, using harsh tones, pushing him to get help, valuing others' needs over his, condescending, name calling, ignoring him, comparing, dismissing.

There are many others. Which ones do you notice that you are doing? Which ones is he doing to you? Recognizing the ways you may inadvertently be shaming him doesn't mean you should ignore the ways he may be shaming you. Stopping your own shaming behavior is no guarantee that his behavior will change, but I've found that it often does.

3. Focus on the positive: From "Mr. Mean" to "Mr. Wonderful."

When we become locked into the Fear/Shame spiral, we get locked into negative perceptions: "He's mean, he's inconsiderate, he's angry all the time, he's withdrawn, he doesn't love me, he's sick." **Most women want to help get the "mean" out of their man. They want to "de-mean" him, but end up "demeaning" him. Instead of trying to fix him, focus your attention on the ways he has been wonderful.**

Think back on things he has done that please you, even if they are small things. What we focus our attention on, increases in our lives. If we want our man to be more wonderful, we have to focus on the good things he is doing. Keep a journal of all the good things he says and does. Read it over when you are feeling afraid and discouraged.

Be aware, however, than many men grow up in shaming and demeaning families. They resist praise from their wives because deep inside they don't believe they are good men. You can remind yourself of his good qualities, but ultimately he has to work through his own shame from the past in order to accept that he is truly wonderful.

4. Be the Best You Can Be.

It's relatively easy to be your best when you are getting the best from your partner. It's a lot more difficult when you are getting a lot of irritability, anger, judgment, silence. Here's an exercise that can help. Write down the things that are best about you as a person. Then write what's best about you as a partner. Most women wouldn't write that they are their best when they are fearful, angry, nagging, blaming, shaming, etc. They are at their best when they are honest, compassionate, courageous, accepting, and optimistic. When times are tough and you're tempted to respond with fear or shame, read what's best about you as a person, and as a partner, and let that deeper truth guide your response.

5. Instead of Having a Talk, Write a Love Letter.

For year's my wife and I have used a "love letter" process that we learned from John Gray. When you're feeling a lot of negative emotions in your life, write a letter to the person who seems to be triggering them. You're not going to give it to the person, so use whatever language best conveys your feelings. "Dear_____".
Then write down any *hurt* and *pain* you are feeling. Next, write down any *anger* or *irritation* you feel. Go on to write things that trigger your *anxiety* and *fear*. Continue with whatever causes you to feel *guilt* and *shame*. Finally, write about your *love* and *understanding*.

Most of us either deny our feelings or we get stuck on one level or another. We get locked up in our hurts or our anger. The letter allows you to express the whole range of your emotions in a safe way. (For a more detailed description of the "love letter" exercise see Chapter 13.) People tell me they always feel better after writing one, and they don't have to say anything to the man, or even give him the letter.

Let me close by saying that I'm *not* suggesting that talking with your partner will always trigger shame or that you should never talk. I am saying that there are a lot of ways we can heal, even when our partner does not want to "talk about it." You'll find as you act on these practices more, and talk less, the emotional climate will thaw and you'll eventually be able to talk without triggering more fear and shame.

Use this space to write out your experiences. In what ways have shame and fear interacted in your relationship? Has talking helped or has it increased the distance between you? In trying to take the "mean out of him," to "de-mean" him, could you be de-meaning him? What actions will you take to change the shame/fear dynamic in your relationship?

NOTES

NOTES

Chapter 23: How Do I Reduce the Stress So We Can Find Some Peace in Our Lives?

Dear Dr. Jed,

I just received your newsletter. It really sounds like my husband may have IMS. Three months ago he told me he hasn't been happy for 2 or 3 years. He has been extremely irritable, short-tempered, and mean. We've both been under a lot of stress lately and I know it has had an effect on our relationship.

We're both busy professionals. He's a physician and I'm an emergency room nurse. We love our work, but it's getting increasingly difficult to practice. Budget cuts at the hospital put pressure on everyone. He also had major surgery on his shoulder two years ago and he hasn't been the same since. Physically, he's fully recovered, but he seems frightened that something else will happen. He tells me he feels like his body is falling apart, even though he's perfectly healthy.

In addition my mother has been sick and I have spent a lot of time trying to take care of her. Both she and my Dad are getting older and I'm worried that their medical bills are going to wipe them out financially and they'll be dependent on us.

Well, I'm rambling on here. You get the idea. I feel that if we can reduce the stress in our lives or deal with it better, we could get back to our old selves where we were a team. Now it's like we're always fighting each other. Help! RT.

Stress is when you are worried about getting laid off from your job, or worried about having enough money to pay your bills, or worried about what kind of future your children will have, or whether your parents will be dependent on you as they age. In fact, for most of us, stress is synonymous with worry. If it is something that makes us worry, then it is stressful.

However, our bodies have a much broader definition of stress. To our body, stress is synonymous with change. It doesn't matter if it is a "good" change, or a "bad" change, they are both stressful. When you find your dream home and prepare to move, that is stress. If you get a divorce, that also is stress. Good or bad, if it is a change in your life, it is stress as far as your body is concerned.

Even imagined change is stress. If you fear that you will not have enough money to pay your rent, that is stress. If you worry that you may get fired, that is stress. If you think that you may receive a promotion at work, that is also stress (even though this would be a good change). Whether the event is good or bad, imagining changes in your life is stressful.

Stress is part of life. If there were no changes in our lives, we'd either be dead or wishing we were. **The problem with stress arises when we have too much change, in too short a time, with too few ways to release and relax.** For most of human history stresses were few and far between. Occasionally, a wild animal would leap out of the forest and we'd have to fight for our lives or run for our lives. Our bodies, minds, and spirit are built for *fight or flight*.

But modern-day stress is primarily psychological, not physical. We are bombarded by worries. We are frightened by angry drivers who wave their fists and fingers at us. We are frustrated at the state of the economy and the inability of our government to provide decent health-care.

However, the body doesn't know the difference between an attacking leopard and a criticizing husband. It can't even tell the difference between a real threat and an imagined one. When stress strikes, whatever the source, the body mobilizes, thinking it's under attack. The body reacts with an outpouring of hormones (i.e. adrenaline, norepinephrine, and cortisol) that increases heart rate and respiration, sends more blood to skeletal muscles, dulls pain, stimulates the immune system, and turns sugar and fat into energy.

We used to get physical in response to stress, whether running away or chasing the animal out of the camp. Now stress is almost constant and we stew in our own juices. It's no wonder we get irritable and angry. So, what can we do? Here are some tried and true ways for dealing with stress.

1. Get moving immediately.

For millions of years of human history we got moving in response to stress. The best stress-reduction technique we have is movement. It's a simple formula: If you have stress every day (and we all do) you must move every day. Start walking, jogging, dancing, playing ball—anything, but get moving. Find some activity, or group of activities, you can commit to doing every day of your life.

2. Reduce the stress in your mind.

In the world our bodies and mind were designed for, the things to worry about were limited: wild animals, poison plants, jealous husbands (yes, we had them back then, too). Now, our worries are endless: terrorist threats, global warming, economic collapse, losing our jobs, our children getting sick, our grandkids starting into drugs, our health deteriorating, and on and on.

Here are two simple techniques to reduce the stress in your mind. First, ask yourself "How are things now?" You'll find the answer is usually, "Fine" or "Pretty good." Worry is always in the future. If you stay in the present, you'll eliminate a lot of stress.

Second, ask yourself, "Do I plan to do anything about this today?" Most of us worry about things that will never happen or aren't really that important to us. If you're not going to do something about the nuclear threat, or global warming, or your kids, or parents, *today*, quit worrying about it. If there is something you can do, do it. When we're *doing*, we're not worrying.

3. Control the changes in your life.

We live in a world of "a million changes a minute." But the truth is, we can control a lot of it. Here's what you can do. *Turn off the T.V.* You don't need a thousand new images bombarding your brain. Take a break. Do something else. Walk in your garden. Play cards. Read a book.

Stop buying new "stuff" and get rid of the clutter. Look around your house. What do you see? If you're like me, too much stuff. Keep the things that truly bring you pleasure and get rid of the rest. Each time you look at things that don't really nourish your spirit, your brain goes through unrewarding changes.

Cart it out, give it away, toss it! Next time you think of buying something new, ask yourself this question, "Will I still think this thing is wonderful a year from now?" Probably not! Resist the corporate exhortations to buy, buy, buy. Remind yourself you don't need more change.

4. Learn to breathe.

I know you don't often think about breathing. You just do it. But most of us breathe too quickly and too shallowly, particularly when we are under stress. Conscious breathing is a great stress-reducer. Here are two techniques I learned from Dr. Andrew Weil, one of the world's leading experts on holistic health.

Sit in a comfortable position with the spine straight and head inclined slightly forward. Gently close your eyes and take a few deep breaths. Then let the breath come naturally without trying to influence it. Ideally it will be quiet and slow, but depth and rhythm may vary.

- *To begin the exercise, count "one" to yourself as you exhale.*
- *The next time you exhale, count "two," and so on up to "five."*
- *Then begin a new cycle, counting "one" on the next exhalation.*

Never count higher than "five," and count only when you exhale.

You will know your attention has wandered when you find yourself up to "eight," "12," even "19."

Try to do 10 minutes of this form of meditation.

Here is another breathing exercise from Dr. Weil that you can do anywhere at any time.

Although you can do the exercise in any position, sit with your back straight while learning the exercise. Place the tip of your tongue against the ridge of tissue just behind your upper front teeth, and keep it there through the entire exercise. You will be exhaling through your mouth around your tongue; try pursing your lips slightly if this seems awkward.

- *Exhale completely through your mouth, making a whoosh sound.*
- *Close your mouth and inhale quietly through your nose to a mental count of four.*
- *Hold your breath for a count of seven.*
- *Exhale completely through your mouth, making a whoosh sound to a count of eight.*
- *This is one breath. Now inhale again and repeat the cycle three more times for a total of four breaths.*

Note that you always inhale quietly through your nose and exhale audibly through your mouth. The tip of your tongue stays in position the whole time. Exhalation takes twice as long as inhalation. This exercise is a natural tranquilizer for the nervous system. Unlike tranquilizing drugs, which are often effective when you first take them but then lose their power over time, this exercise is subtle when you first try it but gains in power with repetition and practice. Do it at least twice a day. It's simple, but takes awhile to perfect.

Once you develop this technique by practicing it every day, it will be a very useful tool that you will always have with you. Use it whenever anything upsetting happens - before you react. Use it whenever you are aware of internal tension. Use it to help you fall asleep.

5. Remember, "You Are Not the Target."

In 1963 Laura Archera Huxley, wife of Aldous Huxley, wrote a wonderful book, *You Are Not the Target*. If offers one of the most helpful techniques I've ever found for reducing stress and turning negative energy into positive. I've given many copies away over the years, but keep my original. Her technique is simple, but effective. I have been using this 4-step process for the last 45 years:

Step 1: Remind yourself that you are not the target.

When your husband complains—
When your boss is irritating—
When your friends are neglectful—
When your business partner is difficult—
When your child is unmanageable—

*Stop! Realize that their irritability, irrationality, lack of consideration, coolness—in other words, their disagreeable and wounding behavior is not really aimed at you. You may feel as though it were, but in the majority of cases it is not. You are **not** the target. You just happen **to be** there.*

Step 2: Decide which part of your body you wish to beautify and strengthen.

We all could use some body toning. Pick a spot—abdomen, buttocks, genitals, chest, thighs, upper arms? Where would you like to use the negative energy coming your way to create a positive change in your body?

Step 3: Move your muscles.

Moving from here to there is helpful, but so is making our muscles move while we're standing still. Contract and relax the muscles of the chosen part of your body in regular rhythms until you find the rhythm that is most comfortable for you. *Now, contract and relax the muscles in your abdomen, buttocks, or wherever, while repeating to yourself, "I am not the target, I am not the target."*

Step 4: Heal the past.

The reason the words from our spouse, boss, or friend hurt so much is that they stimulate memories (often unconscious) from the past. After the unpleasantness in the present has passed, and you can take some time alone, see if you can remember an incident from the past that was triggered by your present situation. You may remember something your father or mother said or did, for instance. *Relive the moment of unpleasantness, and as you feel the bolt of energy flying in your direction, immediately convert it into that rhythmical contraction and relaxation.* If this is too stressful to do on your own, you may want to work with a good therapist.

Use this space to write down your thoughts and feelings. What are the things that are causing stress in your life? What can you do to better handle these stresses?

NOTES

Chapter 24: How Do I Get Through to Him When He Refuses to Admit He Has a Problem?

Dear Dr. Diamond,

My husband is forty-six years old and we have been married for twenty-two years. Shortly before our anniversary this past August, I noticed he seemed distant and somewhat irritable, and for him, almost nasty. Our marriage up until then had been rather ordinary. I thought the reason for his mood change was due to stress, mostly financial, but I assumed things would be O.K.

When I finally approached him about it, he told me he was fine and nothing was wrong. I took the IMS quiz on-line and based on the way I saw him, he scored very high. I know he's got many of the symptoms of IMS. How do I get through to him? I desperately want to help him. But whenever I bring anything up, he just avoids me. Should I just wait until he recognizes he has a problem or should I push harder to get him to acknowledge that something is wrong? BL.

Ninety percent of the men who are going through IMS don't recognize that there is a problem. When asked, they will usually deny that anything is wrong. If pressed, they will withdraw or lash out. Most spouses of IMS men feel they are caught in a bind. "I feel I'm damned if I do and damned if I don't," a 56-year-old woman, married to an IMS man told me. "If I try to help him recognize there is a problem, he resists me and things get worse between us. If I ignore the problem, things just get worse and I feel that I keep getting emotionally battered. What can I do?"

Although this is one of the most difficult aspects of IMS it is not insurmountable. Here's how to begin. Remember the "Chinese finger trap" we played with when we were kids? They were little tubes made out of bamboo braids. We'd stick the index finger from our left hand in one end and the index finger from our right hand in the other. Then we'd try and get our fingers out by pulling. The harder we pulled, the tighter the trap would become. Remember? If not, imagine. The only way to "get loose" was to relax and move the fingers towards each other. As the braids relaxed their grip, we could easily slide our fingers out.

Starting with this little image, here are the steps to get through to a man who is in denial about the impact of IMS on your lives:

1. Take a deep breath, relax, and move towards the problem.

Our initial tendency is to ignore the problem or failing that try immediately to fix it. But like our experience with the Chinese finger trap, the harder we try to fix things, the tighter things become and the more he resists. When I say move towards the problem, it will usually involve moving towards the pain at first. When he acts mean and nasty, rather than ignoring or resisting, take a deep breath and go right into it. Feel the pain, accept what is going on, don't try and force things to be different.

"I couldn't imagine moving toward the pain," one woman told me. "It seemed the opposite of what was needed. But the more I relaxed and let his anger wash over me without resisting, I felt a little freer and could move ahead and do something more effective. I also could recognize his pain and just be open to what he was experiencing."

2. Think about helping yourself, rather than helping him.

This is another step that seems counter-intuitive. It's clear that he's frustrated, unhappy, and not himself. You are trained from childhood to put your own needs aside and help a family member in trouble. Resist the temptation to help *him* at this stage. Ask yourself, "What do I need right now to make me feel better?"

"I realized I needed to be around people who thought I was wonderful," Dora told me. "Since his IMS took over our lives, I had become wrapped up trying to help him. It was like we were both prisoners of his problem. Getting out and being with others helped me see that I was OK and gave me hope that I could improve things in my own life, even if I couldn't fix him."

3. Recognize his anger and "meanness" as expressions of his inner ambivalence and woundedness.

Often when women are in pain, you can tell right away. They look hurt. They appear sad. They tear up when they talk. You feel drawn to help and are rewarded by an appreciative response. When men are in pain, they often cover it over. They appear disinterested and withdrawn. Or they "act out" their pain and become irritable, angry, and abusive. You are repelled by their behavior and you want to withdraw or try to get them to stop acting so mean.

Remember males are taught from the time we were kids to ignore pain. We held back our tears when we were young. We played hurt in sports. Emotional pain was suppressed even stronger. We viewed emotional pain as an indicator of weakness. We learned to armor ourselves and "suck it up." We lashed out at those who tried to comfort us, afraid that if we let ourselves be helped, we could fall apart in a puddle of tears.

"I was terrified to let down my guard and let Joanne know how much I was hurting," 54-year-old Joseph told me. "At first I couldn't even let myself know how much emotional pain I was in. The more Joanne tried to help me, the more enraged I became. Deep inside I *knew* if I let myself feel anything, I would totally come unglued and I'd never be put back together. Joanne would see what a wimp I truly was and lose respect for me. I couldn't hold it in any longer. When I finally let a little bit of the hurt out, I was relieved to find that it wasn't as bad as I thought it would be."

When you can feel strong inside and allow him to express his anger and know it won't wipe you out, you'll be better able to feel his woundedness below the surface of his rage. You'll also know how much he wants to open up, but how fearful he is of falling apart. You can reassure him that you'll be there for him and it's okay to open up to you.

4. Act like the Velvet Bulldog. Be gentle, but be tenacious.

You need to understand this is likely to be quite a journey you are going on. This won't be a quick fix. You will have to stick with it and you must be very strong (like a bulldog) and also very gentle (like soft velvet).

This needs to start with taking care of yourself. Even as you begin to turn your attention to him, you always have to come back to you. It won't be easy being good to yourself. Going through this may stir up old feelings from your past. You may remember wounds from your family of origin that will discourage you from self-care. Remember the *Velvet Bulldog*.

You have to ask yourself how committed you are to this relationship. Things won't change quickly or easily. How long are you
willing to work on this, even if you don't see results—a month, 6
months, a year, longer? Set a time you know you can commit to
and then check in with yourself; this will help you stay focused
even when things seem hopeless. Remember the *Velvet Bulldog*.

5. Take things a step at a time. Denial releases its grip gradually
at first.

Remember that 90% of men don't even recognize there is a
problem at first. You can be reeling from the pain of having your
home fall apart and he is totally oblivious. That's often where you
need to begin with him.

- "Everything's fine," he says. "I don't see any problem here."
- If you're hearing this sentiment, you're at **step 1.** This is your
  chance to breathe deeply, reach out to others, and begin learning all you can about IMS.
- "If there's a problem here, it must be you who has it," he says.
  "If you'd just shape up, everything would be fine."
- "Good," you think to yourself, "now we're at **step 2.**" To him
  you say, "You're probably right. I've got some issues to work
  out." To yourself you say, "Moving toward the problem rather
  than away from it will free me up."
- "Well, maybe it isn't all you," he says. "If there is something
  going on with me I can fix it, fast."

When you agree that you have issues to work out, you disarm
him and gradually he'll come around to recognizing that he's got
some things to work out himself. Now you're at **step 3**. He'll usually try something simple in the hopes that it will make everything
better. Maybe he'll come home early from work on Friday. He
might try cutting down on his drinking. "If there's a problem, I can
fix it myself—fast," is his mantra.

- "I'm still angry and upset," he says. "Maybe I need to try something else."

At **step 4**, he begins to see that this is more serious than he
thought, but he's still convinced that he can fix it himself. "I've
been taught from an early age that a real man solves his own
problems," a 48-year-old truck driver told me. "I was sure if I had
an anger problem I could solve it myself. I tried counting to 10
before I answered my wife. I tried getting my anger out by going to

the gym and pushing iron. These things worked for awhile, but eventually I realized I was still getting upset more often than I should."

- "Maybe I need to talk to someone," he says. "But there's no one who would really understand what's going on for me. And besides counselors take your money and don't really help you."

At **step 5**, he begins to recognize that his problem may require some outside help, but he is resistant to reaching out and telling a stranger what is going on with him. Often talking to a clergyman, a close friend, or co-worker can help break the ice. Once he opens up with someone, he usually finds he has a lot he wants to say, and having someone who understands becomes a higher priority for him.

- "I would like to see a professional."

When a man first comes to see me (or another professional) he is usually quite fearful and ambivalent. He recognizes he needs help, that he can't solve the problem himself, but he wants a "quick fix." It's like he's bringing his car in for an oil change and just wants to get it in the door and out again as fast as possible. He's at **step 6** now and is willing to try something new.

- "I guess I'm more complex than my Chevy and I may need more care than an occasional oil change."

At **step 7** he's fully engaged and willing to work on himself. He recognizes that though his spouse may have her own issues, he has to work on his. He begins to understand the way in which IMS has caused problems for him personally and how it has hurt his relationship. He has had some success and wants things to get even better.

The best way you can help the man get through the various steps is to accept him where he is. There's a tendency to try to push him along. It doesn't work that way. He has to recognize the problem himself and be willing to find his own answers. You can help by encouraging him at every step.

He may decide he doesn't need to move to the next step, that the "simple solution" will work. You trying to convince him otherwise will just create more resistance. Life hitting him in the face will teach him that there is more to do.

In this space, write down your experiences. What is triggered inside you when he denies having a problem? What are your greatest fears? What things have you tried to get through his denial? What has worked? What hasn't worked? Remember to be gentle with yourself. If you begin to feel frustrated, take a break and focus on you.

NOTES

Chapter 25: Everything I Try to Do to Make Things Better Just Seems to Make Things Worse. What Can I Do?

Dear Dr. Jed,

I thought you could give some insight on how I can help my husband and save our relationship. My husband, fifty-one, has been talking about leaving a twenty-seven-year relationship with me after obsessing for a year or so about a woman slightly older than him who has been pursuing him. He sounds and acts totally unlike himself.

I thought we had a good marriage and I don't understand his sudden infatuation with this woman. She's totally unsuited for him. She's clingy and needy—all the things he's always hated. She isn't even very attractive.

He and I have enjoyed a good sex life, but over the past year he has basically excluded me and seems to be thinking of this other woman all the time. He has lost interest in his hobbies, seems to have lost his spirit, and basically seems depressed.

It's obvious that he needs help and he even seems to want me to do something, but everything I try just makes things worse. If I leave him alone he seems irritated and unhappy. When I try and offer suggestions, he resists me. I love him and I know this other woman is just a passing fad, but I don't know what I should do. Can you help? AL.

For many women, the mid-life changes going on with men seem totally incomprehensible. Even when they get over their shock that he's gotten interested in someone else or is thinking about leaving, his behaviors don't make sense. "I could imagine him becoming attracted to a younger, prettier, or engaging woman," his wife told me, "but why would he get involved with someone who is none of these things." They also want to be helpful, but it seems that everything they try to do to improve things has the opposite effect.

I've found that there are six common strategies that most women try. I'll detail what they are, why they don't work, and what you can do that *will* work.

1. The first is to ignore the problem, hoping it is temporary and will soon improve.

For many women the changes are subtle and gradual, and it's easy to miss them in the day-to-day stresses of life. For others, they suspect something is wrong, but they go along with the man when he says that things are fine, that nothing is wrong. Some see warning signs, but they misread them. "He couldn't be getting involved with *her*, she's totally not his type." Others know something is wrong, but they are so invested in the marriage and so fearful of the possibility of losing it, that they simply deny the reality.

Whatever your reasons for ignoring the problem, the truth is that it won't go away and you will have to deal with it sometime. Some people can go on for months and years telling themselves that things will get better tomorrow, but that hoped-for tomorrow never comes.

2. The second strategy is to try harder to be nice, while he continues to be mean.

Many of us, particularly women, are trained to be helpful and supportive. When your partner is obviously in pain, you want to make things better. You may be very tuned into the stresses that he is experiencing, and you believe that you need to go out of your way to be understanding. You find yourself justifying his negative behavior. "He's just under a lot of stress," you tell yourself. "He didn't really mean what he said when he got mad and called me a 'bitch.' If I can just let him know how much I love him, we'll get through this." You find yourself walking on eggshells, trying to smile through your pain, hoping that your care and comfort can heal his wounds. You may find yourself making excuses to family and friends. You feel angry and ashamed at how he treats you and others, but you try to make the best of a bad situation. He may get particularly nasty towards one of the children. You feel caught between wanting to support your child and trying to be supportive to your husband.

Often the more you try to be caring and understanding, the more he accuses you of *not* caring and being unsupportive. It seems you are damned if you do and damned if you don't. And his anger boils up unexpectedly as a result of some insignificant infraction or from nothing at all.

3. The third strategy is to blame yourself.

After being criticized and blamed for everything from putting on weight to being less available for sex, from not being supportive enough to being too involved with his life, you begin to think that maybe he is right. You know you aren't perfect and you have been overwhelmed with things lately. You begin to question yourself. "Maybe he's right," you think. "He's so sure I've done all these terrible things to him. There must be some truth to what he's saying."

While you certainly aren't perfect, and we all have our faults, you need to remind yourself that Irritable Male Syndrome is not caused by something you did or didn't do. Let me say it again: IMS is not your fault, anymore than him becoming depressed or having a heart attack is your fault. Stop it! Blaming yourself doesn't help you, doesn't help him, doesn't help your relationship, and doesn't help your family.

Remember he's feeling terribly confused and frightened. He's looking for something to justify to himself why he is feeling so miserable. It's easier (at least at first) to make you the scapegoat than to turn his attention inward to begin to uncover the real cause of his distress.

4. The fourth strategy is to blame him.

You don't understand why or how, but it's clear that he's changed. He acts like a real S.O.B. He's become disrespectful and mean. Sometimes you let him know directly what you think of him. At other times you make sarcastic comments that you know cut him to the quick. But hey, he started it. Maybe giving him a dose of his own medicine will wake him up. Well, it won't. It will just make you feel as lousy as he does.

When you're bombarded by his judgments and his blame for things that so obviously are not your fault, it's understandable that you would react and fight back. No one likes to feel like a doormat, and you can only take so much. When we don't understand what's going on, we often feel the other person is either *bad* or *mad.* They either seem like they are just being bastards or they must be crazy. "After sucking up his abusive demands I couldn't take it anymore," one woman told me. "I finally just let him have it. I felt some relief for a little while, but it didn't last. I didn't like how it made me feel and I could see that it just made him dig in deeper."

5. The fifth strategy is to try to get him to change.

Most women tell me that they just want their old husband back. They are sure some demon has inhabited his body, mind, and spirit, and if they could just get him to change into the man he was, everything would be all right. They search the web, read everything they can, look for the magic key that they can insert to change him back to the man they've known and loved.

I can certainly sympathize with that desire. It tears you up to see your mate so angry and upset, and you feel increasingly devastated at the impact his behavior is having on you and the family. The problem with trying to change him is this. Inside his psyche he is already feeling like he's coming unhinged, that he's falling apart. From your perspective you want to fix him back up. From his perspective you are trying to take away the last thread of stability that he is so desperately trying to hold on to.

You are sure that if only you could get him the help he needs, things would return to normal. You drop hints and you tell him directly that he needs to see someone—a doctor, a therapist, a counselor, a priest—anyone who can help him get well. You don't really think you're trying to change him, only to help him. It doesn't work. He just feels more pressured, more afraid, and more resistant.

6. The sixth strategy is to change yourself to become the person you think he wants.

He clearly seems to be distancing himself, physically and emotionally. You're frightened and at times panicked. He keeps telling you, sometimes directly and sometimes indirectly, that you are the cause of his problems. He may have gotten involved sexually or emotionally with someone else. Or he may just be seeing you as someone he doesn't want to be around.

You decide that you will make a concerted effort to win him back. You think that if you could lose weight, be more available, dress sexily, be adventuresome, or more responsive to his needs, he will turn back towards you and want you again. No, no, and no! First, changing yourself to please someone else will make you miserable. Second, he doesn't really know what he wants. As soon as you change one way, he wants you to be the other way. One minute he is the nice and helpful Dr. Jekyll. Without warning, however, he changes into the angry and aggressive Mr. Hyde. Third, there is nothing you can change about yourself that is going to fix his IMS. That is something he has to do on his own.

WHAT DOES WORK?

After hearing about the things that won't work, many women feel totally discouraged. "I just felt like giving up," a woman client acknowledged. "As long as I had something to do I felt some glimmer of hope. Even though the things I was doing weren't working, I thought maybe if I kept trying I'd hit on something."

We live in an "action oriented" culture. Men have been trained from childhood to solve problems by strong and forceful action. Many women have learned that same style. They see it paying off in the world of work. They're sure it will be as effective at home.

Paradoxically, doing nothing may, in fact, be the best strategy. Giving up may be the road to success. "Don't just do something, sit there," may be your new mantra. Here's why. Although there are a lot of things you can do, as you're finding out in this book, sometimes our fears lead to frantic action, which leads to more fear, and more frantic action. Your man may be experiencing the same thing. Taking a breather and stopping what you're doing, can give you a sense of calm. You'll come to see that this is not the end of the world and you don't have to act immediately to avert disaster. Giving yourself, and your man, some space can allow new thoughts to enter, new perspectives to develop, and new possibilities to occur.

Use this space to write down your thoughts and feelings. Which strategies have you tried? Are there other ones you've tried as well? What does it feel like to imagine "not trying so hard" and giving yourself some breathing room?

NOTES

Chapter 26: Sometimes I Feel As Mean and Ugly as Him. Is There Such a Thing as "Irritable Female Syndrome"?

Dear Dr. Jed,

I read your book, The Irritable Male Syndrome, and it described my husband perfectly. We're both in our late 40s. We've been married 26 years and our two kids are in college. However, we've both become hypersensitive and irritable. I didn't realize that men could have these kinds of emotional ups and downs. I used to get "crazy" when I had my monthly cycle. PMS drove us all up the wall.

You likened PMS in women to IMS in men. I think you're right about that. But what I'm experiencing now isn't PMS. It's like I'm on edge all the time. I know I'm going through Menopause and that's part of what is going on. With both of us going through this, it's really rough. We're like two caged animals at each other's throats. What can I do to keep from wrecking a relationship that it's taken us years to build? PL.

I specialize in men's health issues. My primary professional focus for the last 45 years is to help men and the women who love them. I wrote the books, *Male Menopause* and *Surviving Male Menopause* because it was clear to me that women weren't the only ones who went through a "change of life."

Before I began my research I assumed that the male change of life would be very different from that of women. I imagined chapters where we'd have the male changes on one side, kind of like the "men are from Mars mid-life changes," and the women's changes on the other side, the "women are from Venus mid-life changes."

However, that's not what the research showed. When we gathered the data it was clear that men and women were much more similar than different. The idea that women's changes were more hormonally and physiologically based, while men's changes were more psychological and socially based wasn't true. One woman in the study said she'd believe there was such as thing as "male menopause" when I could show her men having "hot flashes" (implying that was as likely as showing her that pigs could fly). In fact, a significant number of men, between 25% and 40%, did have hot flashes and their descriptions of the sudden onset, extreme sweating, and disorientation were exactly the same as what many women described.

The impetus for writing *The Irritable Male Syndrome* began with my research on mid-life men; it showed that 80-90% of them were experiencing increased irritability and anger. The most popular articles were focusing on the sexual changes men were experiencing, loss of libido and erectile dysfunction. As with so many perceptions, there seemed to be a gender bias. Sexual changes were *supposed* to happen to men as they aged. Men's emotional ups and downs were invisible. Emotional fluctuations, well, that was what women experienced.

Based on research I had conducted with over 30,000 males, I found that (1) hormonal fluctuations, (2) changes in brain chemistry, (3) increasing stress, and (4) confusion about the male role, all contributed to irritability, anger, and conflict in relationships. But since the book came out, both women and men have often asked me if there is an "irritable female syndrome."

I'm convinced that there is. Men aren't the only ones who go through these kinds of changes. Women, too, have hormonal fluctuations, changes in brain chemistry, increasing stress, and confusion about their roles.

One of the most difficult periods of life for men and women is mid-life, that time roughly between the ages of 40 and 60 when major changes in our bodies, minds, and spirits usher in a new stage of life. Menopause for women and Andropause for men have many similarities. Irritability and anger are things, I believe, we share at this time of life.

My wife, Carlin, and I have both gone through this change. Both of us had long periods where we were hypersensitive, anxious, irritable, and difficult to live with. Human nature being what it is, of course, it seemed to me that *her* irritability and anger were much more hurtful to me than mine was to her. I'm sure she has the same perception. When we believe we are the victim of someone else's anger, we always feel more wounded. When it is us who does the harm to others, we more often explain our anger as being a justified reaction to what the other person did to us.

MEN'S HIDDEN HURT, WOMEN'S HIDDEN ANGER

When I counsel angry men, I find they are often covering a great deal of hurt, sadness, and pain. Many men grew up being sold that "big boys don't cry," and we were shamed for letting out our hurt and sadness. Anger was seen as a more manly emotion. As a result we may become aggressive when we're really feeling sad and vulnerable.

For women, the opposite is often true. Women are taught that anger is not "feminine." Women who express their anger are accused of being "bitches." They learn that it's okay to act depressed, but not okay to be aggressive. Yet anger is as much a part of being a woman as hurt is a part of being a man.

Louann Brizendine, M.D., in her book, *The Female Brain,* describes "aggression in pink." She says, "aggression means survival for both sexes, and both sexes have brain circuits for it. It's just subtle in girls, perhaps reflecting their unique brain chemistry." Brizendine confides that she almost left the topic of aggression out of her book. "I was lulled into a warm glow appreciating the communicative and social female brain circuits. I was nearly fooled by the female aversion to conflict into thinking that aggression simply wasn't part of our makeup."

I know many women who can be quite cutting and hurtful in their relationships, but deny that they are irritable or angry. They insist that it is really the man who is being aggressive. If they acknowledge their anger at all, they believe they are simply defending themselves or reacting to his insensitivity.

Mid-life, when men are going through andropause and women are going through menopause, can be a particularly difficult time for women. "Irritability, lack of mental focus, and fatigue can be caused by low estrogen and made worse by lack of sleep," says Brizendine. These changes may have a negative impact on relationships. "If you don't sleep well for several days," she warns, "it can be hard to concentrate; you may also become more impulsive and irritable than usual and say things you wish you hadn't. So this may actually be a good time to bite your tongue in order to protect relationships."

Double Menopause: What to Do When Both You and Your Mate Go Through Hormonal Changes Together

Given that most couples are within four years of each other, it's not surprising that both will be going through the change of life, more or less, at the same time. This can lead to greater understanding and compassion for yourself and your partner. Or it can lead to the "shame and blame game" where we see our partner as going out of their way to attack us, while we feel like the misunderstood victim.

For years Dr. Nancy Cetel treated men and women with hormonal imbalances. She also taught a popular seminar, "Menopause: His, Hers, and Theirs." After continuing requests from her clients and patients she wrote a groundbreaking book, *Double Menopause: How to Keep Your Romance and Sex Life Alive and Thriving.* In the book's introduction she describes an experience that is similar to thousands that I have had over the last 25 years. "A well-established midlife couple with everything to be grateful for—a beautiful family, a cozy home, a comfortable lifestyle—and a divorce proceeding heatedly under way. Another midlife marital casualty. Not only was I observing this disturbing trend in my practice, but I saw friends' marriages disintegrating after 20 years of love and harmony."

In her chapter titled "Dueling Hormones," she says, "As a gynecologist and reproductive endocrinologist, I believe hormones make the world go around. And when they are out of whack, so, too, is our personal world."

What Can You Do?

<u>1. Embrace Your Anger.</u>

Too many women come to believe that anger is a bad thing, that it is "unfeminine" or "destructive." We get angry when we sense there is a threat to something we hold dear. Anger is good. Anger is natural. Anger is definitely "feminine."

For too long we've bought into the belief that we must avoid anger. As John Lee says in his book, *The Anger Solution,* "Everyone from parents to teachers and pastors have been telling children things like, 'Good girls and boys don't get angry,' for generations. And what about, "it's not ladylike." Girls have been told they are bitches, ball busters, nags, hags, and witches, if they get angry. Boys have been taught to think of 'angry' women that way. We wonder why women are angry—well, just look at what they are called when they express their emotions."

Don't let anyone, particularly yourself, take your humanity away from you. The first step towards dealing with "irritable female syndrome" is to accept your anger as part of being a human being. You may be expressing your anger in a way that is not helpful, but it isn't your emotion that is the problem, it's what you are doing with your anger.

2. Recognize that you are rarely angry for the reason you think.

Most of us believe that other people make us angry. He does something, or doesn't do something, and we react with anger. We may tell ourselves that we shouldn't be angry, or that we shouldn't express our anger, but we still believe it is caused by something or someone "out there."

One of the things that women tell me drives them up the wall is men's silence. "I know something is wrong," a woman client tells me about her husband. "But when I ask him what is bothering him, he says, 'nothing.' It makes me SO mad." What really makes us angry is what we tell ourselves in response to what someone says or does. The thoughts may happen very quickly and it may take some doing to recognize them, but they are there.

What makes a woman so mad when her man tells her nothing is wrong, but she knows something is? It's not his silence, but what she tells herself with thoughts like the following: "If he doesn't talk about it, I'm afraid he's going to explode later" or "When he says nothing is wrong I know he is lying and I hate it when people lie to me" or "If I can't get him to talk about it, I'm afraid our marriage will slip away." What are some of the thoughts that go through your mind, just before you get angry?

3. Understand that anger is tied to unmet needs.

Instead of thinking to yourself, "He's making me angry," try looking inside to see what needs of yours aren't being met. Next time you get angry try filling in this sentence. "I'm feeling angry because my need for _____ isn't being met." You'll often find that your needs for intimacy, care, respect, understanding, safety, or security aren't being fully met.

4. Remember that anger is not the same as blame.

When we were growing up, most of the time anger was expressed in the form of blame. When our father or mother got angry, they were angry at *us*. We were told directly, or indirectly, that we did something *wrong*. They let us know that the punishment we received when they were angry was because we were *bad*.

Once we accept anger as a feeling, without making someone else responsible for our anger, we can stop blaming others (or blaming ourselves).

5. Open up, tell him how you feel, what needs aren't being met, and what you want.

Most of us deal with anger by suppressing it, hiding it, swallowing it, or burying it deep inside. When it does come out, as it inevitably will, it is distorted and often unrecognizable. Many women's anger comes out in passive/aggressive ways. You're not *angry*, but you *accidently* put a dent in the car.

Things will be much better when you open up and tell him what's really going on. You might learn to say something like this: "I'm really angry because I want to feel closer to you and communicate more openly." When he squirms in silence, you might follow up with a request. "Would you be willing to tell me what you heard me saying about my feelings and needs?"

This is a new way to communicate. It will take you some time to learn how to do it. And it will take him some time to learn how to listen and respond. But you'll find it will help you feel better right from the beginning and you will see that your relationship will improve as a result.

In this space, write down your experiences with anger. What things does he say or do that trigger anger in you? What are the thoughts that go through your mind in response? What are you willing to do to be more effective in expressing your feelings?

NOTES

NOTES

Chapter 27: What Are the Things He Should Do Once He Recognizes He Has IMS?

Dear Dr. Jed,

I happened to come across your fine book, The Irritable Male Syndrome, at our local Library. From the thousands of books in the building the title of this book just jumped out at me. I'm half way through reading it and it is wonderful. Thank you for writing it. There are not many books out there like this for us men.

I have had two failed marriages over the past thirty years and often wondered why they went "belly-up" on me. After reading only half of this book little bits of light start to appear and answers are not that complicated. I'm married again and I don't want to go through what I went through in the past. This time I want to deal with these issues before they wreck our relationship.

I'm ready to work to make things better. I just need guidance on what I should do. My wife wants to help, but I don't know what to tell her. Thanks for taking the time to respond. RT.

One of the joys I get in doing this work is seeing people break through their denial and realize that there are things they can do to make their lives more joyful and to have the kind of relationship they long for. It's an interesting, and somewhat mysterious process. For one man, a book jumps out at him at the library, the fog in his mind clears, and he's ready to address these issues. For another man, it's a long and difficult process. He resists and resists and it seems he's never going to be willing to recognize how much IMS is affecting his life. Then one day something shifts inside and he's ready to work.

After helping men, and the women who love them, for more than 40 years, I've come to believe that every man will recognize that IMS is a problem. It's just a question of *when*. Sometimes he "gets it" all at once. Sometimes he gets a little piece of the puzzle at a time. Although each man is different, here are the things that most men do when they recognize IMS has been causing many of the problems that have frustrated them up until now.

1. Breathe a sigh of relief and accept what is.

Before we come to accept that IMS is a problem in our lives, our defenses are up high. We try and convince ourselves that nothing is wrong, or if something *is* wrong it must be someone else's fault. Inside we have a lot of fear—fear of losing control, fear of being overwhelmed with shame, fear of losing our minds, fear of falling apart.

Once we accept that there is a problem, and the problem has a name, *Irritable Male Syndrome,* we can breathe easier. We don't have to spend so much energy repressing our feelings or trying to escape from ourselves. Even if the problems are serious, we can rest assured that we are not alone and things can improve.

2. Recognize that you don't have to solve the problems alone.

One of the reasons most men are reluctant to accept they have a problem with IMS is that we don't know how to solve it. Many of us were raised with the idea that "real" men don't have problems, certainly not emotionally based problems. We are also taught that if we do have a problem, we solve it ourselves. And if we can't solve the problem, we should suffer in silence.

It's usually a great relief when we can finally acknowledge that IMS is a problem for us, and it's an even greater relief when we recognize we don't have to solve the problem by ourselves. If we have a partner, we'll usually find they are quite willing and eager to help, once we stop blaming them and reach out for support.

3. Make amends to those you have hurt.

When we are in the throes of IMS, we say and do things to people close to us that wound them. We often feel so guilty and ashamed we can't acknowledge, even to ourselves, the pain we have caused those we love. Before we can move on, we need to recognize and acknowledge that our actions have been hurtful to others.

This is the time when we can sit down with our spouse or partner and tell them, sincerely, how sorry we are for the pain we caused them. We may also have hurt our kids, damaged relationships with friends, and caused strain with those we work with. Each time we reach out and offer a heart-felt apology we feel a little lighter. If it's possible to right a wrong we've done, let us be willing to do whatever we can to make things right.

4. Make amends to yourself.

Often we are harder on ourselves than on anyone else. We may be yelling and screaming at others or giving them the cold-shoulder, but inside we are telling ourselves one negative thing after another: *I'm no good. I can't do anything right. I hate who I've become. I don't deserve to be happy. I'm a failure.* The litany goes on and on.

For some of us, we've been "talking" down to ourselves for so long, we're not even aware that we're doing it. It's like music that is playing in the background of our consciousness. We may not be consciously aware of what we're saying, but all that negativity goes inside and contributes to our feelings that we are no good.

Just as we have to make amends to others, we need to apologize to ourselves. We need to sit down and have a heart-to-heart with us. Here's what mine sounded like, "Listen, Jed, you've been beating up on yourself for too long. You're not a bad man and you never were bad. It's true you said and did some hurtful things, but you were doing the best you could at the time."

Often the voice of our inner critic will jump in: "The best you could? Hell, you weren't doing your best. You're a shit and you deserve to suffer." We need to gently come back to forgiveness. "No, I don't deserve to keep punishing myself. That doesn't help me, it doesn't help my wife, and it doesn't make things better for my family."

5. Write down the things that trigger your IMS feelings.

There are a lot of feelings that are associated with IMS, but as I discussed in Chapter 16, there are four that are most common: First, *hypersensitivity,* when the least little thing can set us off. Second, *anxiety,* when worry is a constant companion. Third, *frustration,* when we feel hindered or criticized. Forth, *anger,* when the heat rises in us and we tip between keeping the lid on or blowing up.

It takes time to deal effectively with IMS. It helps when we recognize the things that often trigger our reactions. Usually the triggers take us back to some earlier time in our life. Rather than just interacting with those in the here and now, we are actually interacting with *shadows of the past.* It could be our mother, our father, a brother, sister, grandparent, a previous spouse, etc.

John Lee, in his book *The Anger Solution* details the following common triggers:

- Too much

Whenever we get too much of a bad thing, or a good thing, it can trigger us: Too much stimulation, too much to drink, too much food, too much work.

- Too little

When we aren't getting enough of the things we need, it can trigger us: Too little sleep, too little touch, too little nurturing, too little attention, too little sex, too little alone time—are all examples of common experiences of not having enough.

- Certain looks

We've all had the experience of coming home and our spouse gives us that "look." It cuts right to our core. Whatever she's actually thinking, to us "the look" says, "You're screwed up, you're bad, you're going to get it now." Without even thinking about it, we feel like a little kid again getting that look from an angry parent just before the punishment comes.

- Body language

Experts and researchers report that 85 to 95 percent of all communication is non-verbal. Certain body language can trigger our reactions. It can be a turn of the head that triggers body memories of being shamed or disdained. It can be walking away when we're having a disagreement that triggers fears of abandonment.

- Words

The old adage, "sticks and stones may break my bones, but words can never hurt me," tries to take the sting out of hurts we feel when we are spoken to in ways that trigger pain. But the reality is that words are powerful and they can cause us to react, even before our conscious mind registers what has been said. Words that start out with "You always____ You never____ Why can't you just ____" almost always trigger regression to the past and an angry reaction in the present.

- Tone of voice

It isn't just the words that get us, but the tone of voice that goes with them. Often the tone is patronizing, condescending, "holier than thou," rude, critical, or sarcastic.

6. Reduce the stress in your life.

We know that too much stress can trigger all kinds of negative reactions, not to mention what it does to our health and well-being. When we're operating at the edge of our range of tolerance, it doesn't take much to push us over the edge. We often recognize this, but convince ourselves that we can't slow down, can't rest yet, can't take a break.

Well, the truth is we can and we must. Many of us have a tendency to push ourselves, thinking we have to do just a little more or things will really fall apart. I understand how you feel, but nothing is more important than our health and the health of our partner. Once you commit to reducing stress in your life, you'll find that things don't fall apart. In fact you get a lot more done when you aren't so on edge all the time. You will be happier, and those around you will be happier as well.

7. Take time to breathe and relax.

Learning how to breathe well can be one of the best stress relievers there is. You'll never be able to remove all the stressors from your life, nor would you want to, but you can make stress less harmful. Here's an exercise I often give my clients. I learned it from Dr. Andrew Weil who has found that this simple exercise can reduce stress and strain a great deal.

Exhale completely through your mouth, making a whoosh sound. Close your mouth and inhale quietly through your nose to a mental count of **four**. Hold your breath for a count of **seven**. Exhale completely through your mouth, making a whoosh sound to a count of **eight**. This is one breath. Now inhale again and repeat the cycle three more times for a total of four breaths.

I've found that doing this three or four times a day can make all the difference in the world about how I feel and how I relate to others. Try it. You'll be surprised at the results.

Use this space to write down your thoughts and feelings. How does it feel to you to have him acknowledge that IMS is a problem? How can you support his efforts and healing? What things can you do to continue your own healing journey? This is a good time to celebrate. Take some time to appreciate yourself and your partner for the hard work you've done on behalf of yourself, each other, and the relationship.

NOTES

Chapter 28: How Can I Prevent IMS From Wrecking Our Marriage and Insure That Our Relationship Survives and Grows Stronger as We Get Older?

Dear Dr. Jed,

I've been married once before, a roller-coaster relationship that ended badly. Now I'm with a new guy and I feel we can have a really good relationship. We're compatible in all the ways that count, and unlike my first husband, he is very open to talking about his feelings. We don't let things fester, but talk them out when things come up.

I read your book, The Irritable Male Syndrome, when I was trying to understand what was going on in my first marriage. It helped, but we learned about it too late to save the relationship. This time I don't want to wait until we have problems. Are there things we can do to head off IMS?

As is true of most other things in life, prevention is lot easier than treatment. But, people being people, most of us have a tendency to wait until there is a crisis before we move into action. That's too bad because there are a lot of things that can be done to prevent IMS. Unlike death and taxes, IMS is not inevitable. There are things you can do now, particularly if you have a willing partner. And a partner is always more willing to work with you *before* things get out of balance and they feel under attack.

Whether you're starting over with a new partner or starting over with the partner you have, there is a lot you can do to keep IMS from wrecking your relationship.

1. Remember that it's never too late to have a healthy childhood.

The truth is that most of us didn't grow up in families where our basic needs were well met. For some of us, a parent was missing either physically or emotionally. For others, there was some level of physical or emotional abuse. Even for the minority who had "two good parents," there were times when they were overwhelmed and stressed out and not available to us when they were needed.

Many of us grew up with a distorted view of our childhood. We denied what was true. Sometimes we denied how much pain we experienced. Sometimes we even denied the joys of our early years. Here's an exercise that can deeply benefit you throughout your life. Write a personal biography of your childhood. I tell my clients to start by describing the lives of their fathers and mothers a year before they were born. What was the world you were born into? Continue by detailing important events and how they impacted you throughout your growing up years. Pay particular attention to traumatic times and joyful times.

Ask other members of your family—siblings, parents, grandparents, aunts and uncles—to share their memories as well. Add to your biography whenever you can. Gather pictures, letters, anything that will contribute to your knowledge of your origins. Throughout our lives, when we are under stress, we will regress to earlier times. The more we know about those times and how they impacted us, the better able we'll be to get through the stress without becoming irritable, angry, or withdrawn.

2. Accept that we all become passive/aggressive when we are under stress.

Most of us are aware of our feelings and reactions when we're angry and aggressive. Our jaws are clenched. Our breathing is shallow. Our brow furrows. Our eyes narrow. Our mouth gets dry. In the study we conducted on Irritable Male Syndrome with thousands responding from all over the world, the following feelings were reported:

- Grumpy
- Angry
- Impatient
- Hostile
- Annoyed
- Touchy
- Jealous

But many men cover over their feelings of passivity and sadness. We are taught that these feelings aren't manly, so we try and keep them locked away. However, we found that most irritable males also reported the following feelings:

- Gloomy
- Negative
- Tense
- Lonely
- Stressed
- Overworked
- Unloved

This is an exercise that is good for both women and men. Go over the above list. For each feeling, give yourself (1) if under stress you experience it rarely or not at all. Give yourself (5) if under stress you experience it most of the time or always. Being aware of both your passive side and your aggressive side can go a long way towards preventing these feelings from getting out of control.

3. Recognize the connection between present feelings and pain from the past.

We all have stresses in our lives that can trigger IMS symptoms. What makes these emotions so strong and difficult to deal with is that they often stimulate old feelings. I call them "shadows of the past." As long as they stay hidden, they influence us below the level of our awareness. The key is to identify these old experiences and bring them to the surface.

Here's a helpful exercise. Look back over the feelings that you noted in #2 above. Which ones got the highest scores? Think back to times when these feelings were triggered. Remember the situation—who was there, what happened, how did you feel?

Now ask yourself, "Does what happened remind me of anyone or anything from my past?" Often, our first reaction is to say, "No," or "I can't remember anything from my past that ties into this."

But take your time and go a little deeper and you'll often find a tie-in with feelings we had growing up. When we're grumpy, angry, impatient, gloomy, negative, or tense; we may remember times when we felt those feelings as a child. Or it may have been a parent who often felt that way. The tie-in may be that the person (or situation) triggering these recent emotions reminds you of a parent, friend, relative, or teacher from the past who elicited similar feelings.

We all go back to the past when we are in certain situations. For most of us just going home for a visit or a holiday can trigger these feelings. One minute we're a middle-aged adult, the next minute we feel like we're a small child being scrutinized by a critical parent. Identifying these connections and bringing them into our awareness can keep us from being trapped by them.

4. <u>Understand that feelings are telling us whether or not our needs are being met.</u>

We share certain basic needs that humans must have in order to survive and thrive. These include **physiological needs** (air, water, food), **safety needs** (physical safety, emotional security), **love and belongingness needs** (care, respect, connection), **self-esteem needs** (feeling good about who we are, doing things that make us feel worthwhile), and **self-actualization needs** (being all we can be, making a difference in the world). If our needs aren't met we suffer. When they are met we thrive.

I've found that feelings are the most important way in which we know how well our basic needs are being met. When we feel joyful, happy, engaged, satisfied; this tells us our needs are likely being met, or we expect that they will be met soon. When we feel sad, down, disconnected, and frustrated; this tells us that our needs are not being met and we don't expect them to be met in the near future.

If we understand how important our feelings are to our lives, we will do a better job of accepting and appreciating them, whatever they are. Some of us try to hide or deny our negative feelings. That would be like pounding the dashboard in our car until the little red light—you know the one that tells us our oil level is low—goes out. When we honor and appreciate our feelings, it allows us to feel gratitude and appreciation when our needs are being met. It also allows us to figure out ways to meet our needs if they aren't being met.

5. <u>Come to peace with the WOMAN in our lives.</u>

Let's face it, whether we are male or female, young or old, rich or poor, we all have had difficulty with certain women. It could be a mother, grandmother, stepmother, sister, aunt, teacher, spouse, lover, ex-wife, or someone else. But women play a big part in our lives, and understanding our connection to these women and to the archetypal female, the WOMAN, is critical in preventing IMS problems from occurring.

The author Sam Keen offers the best description I know for understanding the WOMAN in our lives. In his excellent book, *Fire in the Belly: On Being a Man,* Keen offers the following:

"It was slow in dawning on me that WOMAN had an overwhelming influence on my life and the lives of all the men I knew. I am not talking about women, the actual flesh-and-blood creatures, but about WOMEN, those larger-than-life shadowy female figures who inhabit our imaginations, inform our emotions, and indirectly give shape to many of our actions."

Keen understand the struggle that most men—even strong, creative, independent, men—have with the WOMAN. "If the text of my life was 'successful independent man,' the subtext was 'engulfed by WOMAN.' All the while I was advancing in my profession, I was engaged in an endless, anxious struggle to find the 'right' woman, to make my relationship 'work,' to create a good marriage. I agonized over sex—Was I good enough? Did she 'come'? Why wasn't I always potent? What should I do about my desires for other women? The more troubled my marriage became, the harder I tried to get it right. I worked at communication, sex, and everything else until I became self-obsessed."

The WOMAN we carry inside is often invisible to us. But we can, and must, bring her out of the shadows. Here's an exercise you can do to help you get connected the WOMAN. It's particularly valuable for guys to do, but women can create their own variation. Think of the person who was the "sex symbol" for you growing up. For me, it was Brigitte Bardot in the movie "And God Created Woman." Depending on your age, you will remember your own "sex Goddess." Now, think of the first girl who excited your fancy. For me it was Nancy Wilson in the 5th grade. She stole my heart and stimulated my fantasy life, though I never had the courage to talk to her. Now think of your mother, who she was when you were first born to age six. Finally, think about those qualities that you feel you don't have, but you look for in a woman. For me they are things like grace, charm, elegance, and soft skin.

Put them all together and you'll have a better understanding of the WOMAN within, that shadowy figure who has such influence over our lives. Getting to know her will help you reclaim the power you have given her. It will help you keep from projecting her good and bad qualities onto every woman you try to love.

Use this space to write your feelings and thoughts. Think about the 5 things you can do to keep IMS from undermining your relationship. Which ones would be most helpful to you? Which ones would most interest your man?

NOTES

PART V:

MOVING INTO THE FUTURE

Chapter 29: He's Moved Out, But I Still Love Him. Is There Any Hope That He'll See What He's Missing and Come Back?

Dear Dr. Jed,

My husband has become someone I no longer recognize. He used to be easy going and upbeat, but he's become increasingly sullen and angry. We've been married for 22 years and have three wonderful kids. We've had our ups and downs throughout our marriage, but I think I can say honestly that it's been a pretty good marriage for both of us.

At least I thought it was. Over the last 3 or 4 years there have been a lot more stresses. He changed jobs a couple of times and we've been worried about our future financial stability. We lost a lot when our retirement investments tanked. I've tried to talk to him about these things, but he just gets mad.

I tried to get him to go to counseling, but he said he didn't believe it would help. Three months ago he moved out. He told me he had to sort things out and just couldn't live at home any more. He has an apartment not too far from where he works. He still comes by to see the kids, but he doesn't seem to want to have anything to do with me.

I just can't believe it. I have notes and cards that date as late three months before he moved out telling me how much he adores me. Now he seems like he can't stand me. Some days I want to give up and get a divorce. Other days, I think he'll come to his senses and come home. What should I do? JL.

Is there hope that a man will come back once he moves out? The short answer is "yes." Most often I find that even when the man moves out, there is hope for reconciliation. However, for most of us, having our spouse move out is tremendously painful. When I counsel women in these situations they express a whole range of feelings—shock, anger, hurt, fear, confusion, guilt, shame. They express a range of thoughts as well. "Why is this happening to me, to us, to the family?" "To hell with him! If he doesn't want to be with me then I'm better off without him." "How can he tell me he adores me and three months later move out? It doesn't make any sense." "Is he crazy or am I crazy or are we both crazy?"

Do any of these feelings or thoughts seem familiar to you? After having worked with thousands of couples going through these IMS upheavals, I've concluded that in some ways both the man and his spouse are "out of their minds." They aren't crazy in the sense of being psychotic, but they're not rational adults either. So, what's going on here?

IRRITABLE MALE SYNDROME AND EMOTIONAL REGRESSION

In commenting on their husband's emotional volatility and actions, women tell me that he's not acting at all like himself, like the man they have lived with for years. When I probe more deeply, they tell me he seems to have regressed. "It's as if he's become a rebellious teenager," one woman said. Another told me, "He's throwing tantrums like a two-year old." Another said, "He's like a kid who, when he doesn't get his way, gets red in the face, and leaves home."

One of the first steps to understanding what is going on, and deciding what to do, is to recognize that the stresses of IMS can push a man (or a woman) to regress to earlier stages of life. We see the same thing with children who have experienced some kind of trauma. A five-year-old, for instance, may regress and begin wetting her bed again following the divorce of her parents. Although we recognize regression in children, we often have a difficult time understanding it in adults.

John Lee, author of *The Anger Solution* says, "Emotional regression is one of the best-kept secrets in modern psychology." He defines it as "an unconscious return to our past history." That's important to know and fits what we see in men going through IMS. When he's shouting at you, blaming and shaming, even when he moves out, he's responding more to feelings from his earlier life than he is to things that have gone on in the marriage. "When we regress," Lee reminds us, "we are hurled into our past faster than lightning. We say things or react in the way we did when we were in our twenties, teens, or late or early childhood."

One of the most confusing things about IMS is how quickly a man can change from seeing his wife as his loving partner to seeing her as his enemy. "It's like he isn't seeing *me*," a client told me. "He's seeing someone else, someone dangerous. It's like someone flipped a switch in his brain and he perceives me as an ugly witch"

That description may be quite accurate. There is a classic illusion where we see a picture which looks either like a young woman or an old hag. You can't see both at the same time, but your brain organizes the information so that you see one or the other. Which do you see, an old woman with a big nose or a young woman in profile with a strong chin line?

In some ways this is what happens when we regress. Instead of seeing the beauty in our present life, or our present wife, we see the ugliness from some past trauma. We're projecting onto our present relationship thoughts and feelings that are really from the past.

NULLIFYING THE PAST AND SEEING THE WIFE AS ENEMY

When the man begins to think about leaving, he also starts looking for reasons to justify the inner panic that arises as regressive emotions emerge. Often there is no "real" reason that can justify the strength of his feeling. As a result he often re-organizes the past in his own mind. Where he used to see their life as mostly good, with the usual downs that are part of all long-term relationships, now he begins to see the past as mostly negative.

It's as though his brain flips from "beautiful woman to ugly witch" and he gathers up all the bad memories and forgets all the good ones. Where he used to look back on a life-story of a good marriage and a good wife, he begins to see a bad life and a bad wife. For the wife it's a "crazy-making" experience.

In her book, *Sudden Endings: Wife Rejection in Happy Marriages,* Madeline Bennett, describes the regression she was experiencing with her husband when he moved out of the house. "The third month away he reduced the amount of his check and snarled when I complained," Madeline recounts. "His voice on the phone was hard and icy. I didn't admit it at the time, but he sounded as if he *hated* me. The voice was that of a stranger, the demeanor that of an enemy."

As the panic begins to rise, men often become like confused homing pigeons that fly 180 degrees in the wrong direction. What they really need is to open up and share their feelings with someone who they can love and trust. Instead they think that their loving spouse is really out to harm them, and they must escape before it's too late.

"Among other gyrations," Madeline realized, "when his emotional compass was pointing in my direction, it was no longer pointing toward friend or lover but toward an unwanted intruder." Often old unhealed wounds from childhood get projected onto the spouse. Madeline's husband began to criticize her for doing things she had never done to him, but which she knew *had* been done by his mother and father. "This was only a foretaste of what developed later when his confusions multiplied. I was to be mistaken for his mother, his father, and anyone else who had ever been disloyal to him."

John Lee describes the distortions that occur with emotional regression as "present-person/people erasers." We no longer "see" the person in front of us—our loving spouse or partner—but rather we are projecting old wounds from our fathers, mothers, or other people who have hurt us in the past. We are not living in the present; we are interacting with shadows of our past.

Vicki Stark, in her book, *Runaway Husbands: The Abandoned Wife's Guide to Recovery and Renewal,* offers advice and support to women who are facing the reality of a husband's leaving. Based on her own experiences and the unique research she has conducted, she shows that women can understand why this happened and what they can do to heal.

WHAT YOU CAN DO

1. Deal with the shock of his moving out.

For most people, no matter how stressful the relationship has been, when a spouse moves out we go into shock. There are feelings we must deal with, confusing thoughts to sort out. There is a hole in our lives and in our heart and soul. With a man going through IMS, the changes may be sudden and unexpected. This is a time to "ground" yourself, physically and emotionally.

You need to reach out for friends and family and let them support you. This isn't always easy. A couple splitting up may stimulate divided loyalties. Some people don't want to take sides, so are afraid to offer support for fear it will look like they are siding with one partner over the other.

Nevertheless, you must keep trying until you get a group of people who can be there for you. You may need someone to talk with about how you feel and the thoughts going through your mind. You may need someone to help with the practical things—fixing an appliance, cleaning the yard, hauling away trash. Don't be afraid to ask for what you need.

2. Remind yourself that his moving out doesn't mean the relationship is over.

As I've said, this is a time of turmoil. The man isn't likely to be in his right mind. He's confused and ambivalent. One minute he may say, "It's over. I want a divorce." Then he may change his mind and tell you, "I just need time to sort things out."

This is a time when you must be clear with yourself. Ask yourself, "Is the relationship over for *me*?" If it's not, you need to keep your focus on doing everything you can to support the healing that must occur to bring things back together. Don't go along with *anything* that is not in support of your desire to heal and bring the relationship back together.

3. Let him know that you support him in getting his needs met and you believe things can be healed in the relationship.

You want to support your man's needs for space to sort things out. But you also want to support your own needs to work things out. Remember, he is probably in a regressed emotional state, even though he may believe that he is thinking clearly. He is actually overwhelmed, at times, with old wounds and pain. He may try to protect himself by projecting the past onto you.

You need to hold the healthy, loving, mature position of reconciliation. You should listen to his feelings and needs, but at the same time let him know you are hopeful that things can be worked out.

4. Encourage him to do some counseling with you.

Men often are hungry to talk about what they are going through, but afraid of being overwhelmed by their feelings and fears. Find a counselor who can be supportive and invite your spouse to join you. Don't pressure him, just invite. If he says, "no," go yourself. Try again later.

5. Set a check-in date to re-evaluate progress.

There are two mistakes women often make. They give up too soon or they stay too long. Some women give up on their relationship quickly. They are unable to deal with the pain of rejection or the ambivalence of not knowing how things will turn out. Other women hang on long after it's clear that he isn't going to change and give the relationship a chance.

Don't let anyone—friends, family, even your therapist—convince you to leave if you're not ready, or to stay if you feel you've given it as much time as you are able. Having a check-in time to re-evaluate can help avoid either of these extremes. If it's a three-month check-in, for instance, you would keep your focus on healing the relationship for three months, no matter what he does.

At the end of that time, you'd ask yourself some hard questions. "How do I feel? Am I ready to move on, or do I still have hope that things can get better?" "Is he really taking time to sort things out or has he made up his mind that its over?" "Is he able to break out of his regressions to talk honestly and openly about his feelings and needs?" Based on your answers, you will either decide that it's time to let the relationship go and you'll begin to move on, or you'll see some progress and decide to set another check-in date to look again.

In this space, write down your thoughts and feelings. How do you feel about his moving out? Do you see him regressing and experiencing wounds from relationships in his family of origin? Do you notice any regressions in yourself? How committed are you to making things better and how long are you willing to work to reclaim the relationship?

NOTES

Chapter 30: How Do I Deal With the Effect of IMS on the Children?

Dear Dr. Jed,

When I heard your talk on the radio, I broke down in tears. You were describing my husband, Jeff, like you'd been living in our home for the last five years. He's 45- years-old, we've been married twenty-one years and have three children—age 19, 15, and 9. Jeff is a natural helper, happiest when he is doing things for others.

He has always been a wonderful father. He played ball with our son, went to his practices, and was a coach for many years. Our younger daughter also loves sports. She plays basketball and volleyball; she's tall like her Dad. In the past 6 months, Jeff seems to have forgotten he has children. They want to tell him about their day, share their ups and downs. He used to listen and always understood.

How he buries himself in his books, or he reads the newspaper and grumbles about the state of the world, or he gets lost in his computer. It's like we've become a family of four and Jeff is no longer with us. I miss my husband and it tears me up to see how this is affecting the kids. They are growing up fast and I'm afraid Jeff's neglect will do real damage. What can I do? ML.

One of the saddest aspects of IMS is the impact it has on children and families. Although a man's withdrawal from his spouse may be difficult to deal with, it's even more confusing and hurtful when he withdraws from his family or turns his anger on the children. A woman usually has multiple close relationships that sustain her with family and friends. However, for children the relationships with Mom and Dad are critical throughout their lives. What's going on?

The easiest way to understand the impact of IMS on the family is to recognize that the man has a serious disorder that affects his brain function. Think about someone you know who is seriously depressed, for instance. When the depression is at its worst, the person is withdrawn and/or hostile. They are definitely not themselves. They often hurt the ones they love the most. Or think of a person who has a serious alcohol or drug problem. Their drinking or drug use takes over more and more of their life, and family and friends get pushed aside. Or consider someone who suffers from chronic pain. When in pain, everything and everyone fades into the background. Only the pain is real.

Examining the impact of depression on the family can enable us to better understand IMS, and how to help our children get through this. Depressed men tend to "act out" their pain. It appears to them that other people, particularly their wives and children, have changed and now go out of their way to irritate them. "When I was in the depth of my IMS depression," a 46-year-old father of three told me, "it seemed like everyone was going around scratching their fingernails on the black-board of my brain. For a long time, I thought I was fine, that there was nothing wrong with me. I was sure that *they* had changed. Looking back now, I feel terrible about how I treated them all, particularly the kids. I've got a lot of amends to make and a lot I need to do to heal the wounds I inflicted."

So, what can a spouse do to protect herself and the children from IMS?

1. Calm your fears.

There's nothing that frightens a parent more than to feel that their children are in danger. Nothing hurts more than to see the look on our child's face when they are hurt. And nothing is more painful than to witness our child upset by the actions of a parent. So, this is a time when you have to make extra effort to be calm. You need to remind yourself, "My husband is in pain and he is taking his pain out on those closest to him. We are strong and we can get through this. There are things we can all do to take care of ourselves and those we love."

We have to remember not to panic. We have to remember not to blame ourselves or our partner. Blaming ourselves or our partner for having IMS makes no more sense than blaming ourselves or our partner for having diabetes, depression, alcoholism, or heart disease. They all impact the family and they can all be effectively treated once we understand what to do.

2. Stop and take care of yourself.

When our children are in danger, we automatically reach out to help them. We forget about our own needs and focus on theirs. But that may not be the wisest first move. There's a reason why the safety talk given before every flight tells us: If the airplane should lose pressure, oxygen masks will automatically drop down. Put your own mask on first, then put on the mask your child.

We need to recognize that we can't be of help to our children, or anyone else, if we don't make it. So, take a deep breath. Take some time to take care of you. Then turn towards the children.

3. Educate yourself about IMS.

When I wrote the book, *Irritable Male Syndrome: Understanding and Managing the 4 Key Causes of Aggression and Depression* in 2004, no one had ever heard of this problem. Now a lot of information is available. If you're particularly concerned about your children you may have turned directly to this chapter to get the answers you need now.

This is the time to learn as much as you can. Read the other chapters in this book.

Check out the resource section at the end of the book.

4. Recognize that he is hurting, but feels stuck.

When a man is acting "mean," it's difficult to remember that he is in pain. Remember that his irritability and anger are covering over his hurt and fear. He may act sure of himself, but he is often quite confused. He may seem angry and blaming, but underneath it there is a lot of pain and sadness.

5. Talk to the children.

You want to let them know you are aware that Dad is acting strange, that he has changed in ways that are difficult and confusing to understand. Obviously what you say will depend on their ages. Sometimes we think that small children are too young to be aware of the issues. But the younger the children, often the more intuitive they are. They know something is going on, though they may not understand what it is. They know Daddy is withdrawn or angry or irritable, even though they may not have the words for it.

Letting them know you are aware that something is going on with Dad can be a great comfort to them. You can explain in appropriate ways that Dad is suffering from a serious problem that makes him more hypersensitive, anxious, frustrated and angry.

You may need to remind them numerous times that this isn't their fault, that they haven't done anything wrong, that they aren't "bad." You will also have to remind them (and yourself) numerous times that this can be a difficult problem to treat, but that there are positive things you all can do, even when Dad doesn't yet recognize he needs help.

6. Never listen to what he thinks about you. Listen to how he *feels* and what he needs.

When a man is going through IMS he is often judgmental and blaming. It's hard not to take it personally. For instance, an IMS male may say things like, "Damn it, can't you ever do anything right? Are you really that stupid?" You can think, "I must be a lousy wife." Or the kids can think, "Dad hates me."

Or you can tune into his feelings and say to yourself, "He seems to be frustrated, angry, and enraged. I wonder if he's needing support or care or maybe he needs to rest or relax." It's not easy to tune into his feelings while you feel under attack. But to the degree that you and the children can do that, it will keep you from being overwhelmed, and eventually he will recognize that he's being irrational in the face of care and support.

7. Tell him directly that his behavior is affecting the children.

Most IMS men feel guilty about their behavior, but because guilt makes them feel even worse they deny it. You need to help him to change his behavior without making him feel worse about himself. When he's in a calm mood (or as calm as he gets these days), say something like this, "I know you love the kids very much but you're feeling irritated and angry with them. I know you want their love and respect, and they very much want yours. I understand you're doing your best to treat them kindly even when you're feeling upset, and I support your continuing to do that. They're our kids and hurtful words are hard to take back. I love you and we can work this out."

8. Go for a walk and talk.

Men often open up more easily when they are communicating "side by side" rather than "face to face." Men tend to be "doers." "Honey, we need to talk," is usually the first step towards disaster.

Going for a walk and letting the talk "just happen" often works much better.

9. Don't give up.

Whether you have kids or not, I encourage people to do everything they can to work things out. When you have kids, it's even more important. They need you both, no matter what their age. It's not easy, but with knowledge and support you can do it.

10. Don't take his abuse.

Some women are so afraid that what they say or do will drive him away, they allow him to be abusive to them or the children. Don't let that happen to you. The best thing you can do for yourself, your children, and your man, is to stand up to abuse. You can say, "Henry, I love you (of course if his name is John, it's better to use 'John'), but I won't allow me or the children to be the brunt of your anger. I know you don't mean to be abusive, but sometime you are." These words may be the most difficult you'll ever speak, but they can save your lives.

Here's a chance for you to write down your feelings and thoughts. How has his behavior affected the kids? What have you done to make things better? What will you try now?

NOTES

NOTES

Chapter 31: Can Our Relationship Start Anew Even When It Looks Like It Has Died?

Dear Dr. Jed,

I bought your book on Saturday and stayed up till 1:30 a.m. reading the portions that apply and am now reading it systematically. I cannot describe how much it has helped me to understand the IMS husband I have had for 21 years. It has been so comforting to realize that when everything came to a head I am not the only wife that has gone through this and others felt the same confusion I did.

When I read the account of Donna Rollins it was like reading my own story although my husband went one step further. He had an affair and when I found out about it he moved out. The affair didn't last long, but he hasn't come back. I'm not sure I want him back, even if he decided to return. I'm still reeling from all that has happened in such a short period of time.

I still love my husband and I wonder whether we could rebuild our relationship or if it is truly over. I'm not ready to move on yet. Am I just kidding myself thinking we might still have a chance? Can a relationship be resurrected? TT.

Most of us have a difficult time letting go of a long-term relationship even when it appears to be over. We hold on to a glimmer of hope that the relationship could come alive again. But we also fear that we're just being foolish, setting ourselves up for more pain and suffering. We remember times in the past when we thought, "maybe this time it will be different," only to have our dreams crushed.

On the other side of the coin, many of us have had the experience of ending a relationship and later wondering if we had given up too soon. We see our "ex" and picture the future we might have had if we'd stayed together. We think about family gatherings and what they would be like if the family was still intact.

In working with thousands of men and women who have gone through Irritable Male Syndrome, I have found that many relationships can come alive again even when they've gotten battered, bruised, and buried. It was the great philosopher Yogi Berra who reminded us, "It ain't over 'til it's over." In referring to the game of baseball, he was telling us that no matter how many runs our team may be down, there is still hope until the last past pitch of the last inning has been thrown and the last out has been made.

In referring to life and relationships, I tell my clients, "The relationship is never over until you decide it's over." But what if he tells me, "I want a divorce!" "It's over, right? You can't have a marriage if only one person is committed, can you?" My answer is, "It's never over until you decide it's over." I give them the same answer, when they tell me, "He's had an affair. It's over, right?" And when they tell me, "He's moved out. It's over, right?" And when they say, "He tells me the relationship is dead. It's over, right?" And when they say, "My friends tell me, I have to move on. It's over, right?"

The truth is, no one can tell you that your relationship is dead, but you. That's the good news and the bad news. On the positive side, it means that you have control over your future, not some outside forces that are beyond your control. The bad news is that you have control over your future. There's no one who can decide for you and let you off the hook.

So, if you're ready to take charge of your own life, here are the steps I have found most helpful.

1. Reclaim your intuitive knowing.

When a relationship has been battered by IMS, one of the first casualties is our intuition. Over the years we all develop an intuitive sense of what's going on in the relationship. We have a "gut feeling" when our spouse is lying or withholding information. But over time we come to doubt ourselves. We lose touch with what is true for us.

In order to move ahead with our lives and to make good decisions about our future, we need to get back in touch with that "intuitive knowing" that we all have. So, take a deep breath, close your eyes, and let your attention go inside. Ask yourself, "What do I know for sure about myself and my life?" You may get in touch with answers like this: "I know I'm going to be okay, no matter what happens." "I know I have friends who care about me." "I know I'm a good person and don't deserve to be abused." "I know I want to have joy in my life." "I know I want relationships that are healthy and joyful."

It may take some time for you to get back in touch with that inner core of intuitive knowing. Months or years of neglect may have caused you to disconnect from yourself. But little by little you will come back home.

2. Take an honest look at the relationship with your spouse.

Take out 4 pieces of paper. On the first one write, "These are the positive, healthy things about my relationship." Then write as many things as you can. Let your answers come from both your logical mind as well as your intuitive mind. On the second piece of paper write, "These are the negative, unhealthy things about my relationship." Again write out your answers. On the third piece of paper write, "If I let go of this relationship and move on with my life, these are the positive, healthy things I would be likely to experience." Write your thoughts and feelings. On the fourth piece of paper write, "If I let go of the relationship and move on with my life, these are the negative or unhealthy things I would be likely to experience." Look at your answers. Weigh the healthy aspects against the unhealthy ones.

3. Reach out to a few trusted friends who know you and your spouse.

This is a difficult thing to do. Many of us have kept our relationship problems hidden from even our closest friends. We may have put up a good front because we were ashamed to let others know what was really going on. Yet, our friends generally have a sense of what is going on.

This is a time to talk with a close friend. Tell her (or him) you're sorting out your feelings and thoughts and would them to listen to you. Read what you wrote previously. Ask them if there is anything they can add to the answers you've given to the four questions. Explain that you're not asking them to tell you whether you should let the relationship go or try and rekindle it. You know you need to do that yourself. You simply want their input about how they see the "pros and cons" of your relationship.

4. Consult the ancestors.

When we are young, we have a rather naïve view of relationships. We fall in love with our college sweetheart. We get married and have children because it's what we've dreamed about and what is expected of us. But as we get older we realize there are deeper reasons we choose the relationships we do. There are life lessons we need to learn and our relationships give us the opportunity to become who we are meant to be.

In an ideal world we would have been raised by wise parents who could help us know what is best for us. They would have helped us to understand what lessons we need to learn and what relationships would be in our best interests. Sadly, most of us didn't have ideal parents, but there is wisdom in our ancestors.

I've found this exercise helpful. Close your eyes and let your attention go inside. Ask all your ancestors—your mother, your mother's mother, your father, your father's father—back through time, to give you their wisdom. Let them speak to your intuitive mind, to your heart and soul. Be open to whatever thoughts or feelings come into your awareness. Write down whatever wisdom comes to you about yourself, your life lessons, and your relationships.

5. Decide in which direction you want to go.

Based on all the wisdom you have at hand, decide in which direction you want to go. Do you feel drawn toward your relationship or away from it? Here's another exercise that can help. Close your eyes. Let your attention go inside. Imagine that you're walking on a path in the woods. You feel relaxed and comfortable, safe and secure. You are surrounded by beauty. As you walk along, you approach a fork in the path. You are intuitively aware that if you take the left fork it will take you toward your relationship. If you take the right fork it will take you toward a new life. Without thinking, let your intuition take you either left or right.

Many of us are afraid we'll make a mistake. "What if I choose to try and resurrect the relationship and it doesn't work out? I'll feel awful," you think to yourself. "What if I go the other direction and I end up all alone?" The truth is you can't make a mistake. Whatever you decide, you're always on your life-path. If you decide you want to do what you can to rekindle your relationship, then put your energy into doing that. If you decide to move on, let your heart take you on this new path.

RESURRECTING A RELATIONSHIP

Hans and Heidi Moiler are a couple whose relationship was on the rocks. Heidi first contacted me after her husband had moved out. "He's 50 and I'm 45," Heidi told me. "We've been married nearly 23 years and have had an exciting life together. But about four years ago I sensed boredom setting in, for whatever reason. I felt him withdrawing from me and from our children. He spent more time on the road with his work. He finally told me he didn't want to be married anymore, that he wanted his freedom."

After talking with Heidi for a number of sessions, I spoke to Hans. He agreed to come in to talk, even though he told me he didn't think it would do any good. "In mid January this year I informed my wife that I wanted a separation from our marriage. Since then we have taken a time out in which both of us travelled extensively and the break gave me a chance to see what I really want. My wife would like me to come back and to re-build our marriage. But I think I want to date younger ladies. It makes me feel younger again."

Like many men, Hans was feeling the draw to find a younger woman in order to help him feel younger. I was able to engage him in exploring what he really wanted with his life. Over time it became apparent that he wanted to re-vitalize himself and re-vitalize his marriage, but he didn't know how to do that. It seemed to him the marriage was dead and he had to move on.

I was able to show them both that it was possible to breathe life back into a relationship that they had both cherished but feared was dead. It took Hans some time to realize that it was possible, but once he did, he engaged fully. Over a period of six months they were able to bring their relationship back to life. A year later they each wrote me a note.

Here's what Heidi said: *I came to realize that our individual needs could be met within the relationship, without either of us feeling we were being compromised. In the delicate dance of long term relationships, the steps have now been made much simpler. I feel I've gotten my husband and best friend back again.*

Here's what Hans said: *I finally felt I had come home to the answers to questions that had taken me off course for a few years, from my life of being present with my loving wife and children. I had come very close to discarding the things that meant the most to me. Jed's positive persona was self evident and showed me that I could ease into the second half of life and still be happy. Being a hobby sailor, it was like putting a boat back on north course after sailing through un-chartered waters with plenty of reefs. Today we are enjoying our life with the fullest intensity and it has changed by 180 degrees.*

In this space you can write out your thoughts and feelings. What did you learn about yourself, your relationship, and your future? What direction feels right to you? What can you do to make your life a reflection of your true spirit?

NOTES

NOTES

Chapter 32: How Do I Insure I Don't Pick Another Mr. Mean in My Next Relationship?

Dear Dr. Jed,

I wish I had learned about IMS years ago. By the time I found your book, my husband was long gone. It took awhile, but I finally had to accept the ending of our marriage. It has taken a long time, but the wounds are healing and I feel I'm ready to move on. What worries me the most is that I'll make the same mistake I made the first time.

I thought we had a good marriage. When he began to withdraw I thought it was just the stresses he was experiencing at work. I was sure things would return to normal. Even after he had the affair, I thought we could work things out. I knew we loved each other and I thought love would be enough to save us. But he became a different man, not at all the caring, involved man I married.

I don't know whether he had these IMS qualities all along and I missed seeing them or if he developed them once we were together and I missed seeing them. Is there something about my personality that attracted a Mr. Mean? What can I do to be sure I don't fall into another relationship like the last one? I can't stand the thought of going through that kind of pain again. Can you help me? LC.

Many women find that with knowledge and understanding they can heal their IMS relationship and their marriage can grow even stronger and healthier. For others, they address the problems too late or the problems are so deeply engrained that the only way to move ahead with their lives is to get out of the relationship. They have to finally let go, grieve the loss, heal the wounds, and get back in touch with their own heart and soul.

It takes time to heal, months for some, years for many. But at some point you are ready to reach out again in the world. You long for a relationship that can be truly fulfilling. But as your desire for connection begins to emerge, so, too does your fear. You recognize that regardless of the changes that may have gone on in your previous relationship, you chose the guy. No one forced you to be with him. You don't want to make another bad choice. What do you do? Here are my best suggestions.

1. Examine the wound in your love map.

The idea that each of us has a specific "love map" that determines who we become attracted to was developed by psychologist and sexologist John Money. According to Money, "There is a rather sophisticated riddle about what a boyfriend (or girlfriend) and a *Rorschach inkblot* have in common. The answer is that you project an image of your own onto each. In many instances, a person does not fall in love with a partner, per se, but with a partner as a Rorschach love-blot."

Few of us grew up in a family where we received all the love, affection, and support we needed. Most of us experienced some wounds to our love map. We may have had an alcoholic father who we longed to connect with, but who was absent physically or emotionally. We may have had a mother who was very critical of how we looked or of our accomplishments.

We pick a partner, often unconsciously, because we hope they can give us the love we missed. We hope they can fill the holes in our love map, so we can be whole. Knowing where our wounds are can help us recognize where we may be vulnerable. Many of us are blind to unhealthy relationships if the person seems to offer a "fix" for those early wounds.

2. Understand the unconscious need to re-create the wounding relationship.

Whether we are conscious or unconscious of the wounds in our love maps, most people make a conscious effort to find a partner who is unlike the wounding parent. "My father was an alcoholic," a 52-year-old female client told me in one of our first sessions. "He wasn't a mean drunk, but I could never count on him for anything. He would promise to come to a school event, but he'd end up stopping for a drink and would be late or miss it altogether. One of the things that attracted me to my husband was that he didn't drink, seemed super-responsible, and thought I was wonderful."

My client was totally surprised when after years of marriage she began to see that her husband, in fact, had a lot of the same qualities as her father. "He never drank a lot, but he would always have a few drinks after work," she told me. "Although he appeared to be very responsible and totally supportive of me, it soon became evident that he was very focused on his own career, his own needs, his own desires. He was really wrapped up in himself, just like my father."

In working with men and women over a lot of years, I came to recognize a psychological pattern that helped explain why people picked partners who were abusive in the same ways as their parents even though *consciously* they were choosing someone quite different.

If we would get the unconscious mind to explain it, we might hear the following: *In order to heal the wounds from my family, to get the love I didn't get from my Mom or Dad, I have to re-create the same kind of emotional environment I grew up in. But where I failed in the past to get my parents to love me and give me what I needed, this time I'm going to succeed. This time, I'll get my husband to give me what my father never could*

The essential desire is a positive one. We do need to heal from our early wounds. The problem is that as we create the same conditions, we bring about the same results. Since we are unconscious of the fact that we've married our father (or mother) we aren't able to bring new skills to the situation. Making the unconscious, conscious, can free up our energy to heal and move on with our lives.

3. Accept that whatever parental love you received is all you're ever going to get.

Whether we are aware or not, most of us are still looking for the parental love we never received as children. We often "fall in love" when we think we've found it, then become disillusioned when we aren't being given to in the way we had hoped. We give to others in the hopes that they'll give back to us.

It's one of the most difficult, yet healing life-lessons, when we finally realize that whatever amount of love we got from our parents is all the parental love we're ever going to get. Once we accept that, we can stop trying to get something from a mate that we'll never get. It also relieves us of the burden of trying to make up for what a spouse didn't receive.

We can then spend more time being grateful for what we did get. Our parents gave us life. We were given some lessons that we had to learn in order to survive and thrive. We can forgive them for their limitations and forgive ourselves for not doing better. Paradoxically, accepting that we'll never get enough, frees us to actually receive more of the abundance of the love that is all around us.

4. Stop looking for your "soul-mate" or perfect partner.

Part of the fairytale we all grew up with is that we would find "Prince Charming" or that magical someone who would make our life complete. Once you let go of believing there is one person who will fill all the gaps you feel inside, you can let go of finding that "special someone."

We think we're being selective, that we're waiting for the person we can "fall in love with." In truth, we're waiting for someone who doesn't exist. Forget finding a soul-mate and look for someone who will be a good friend and life companion.

5. Open your heart, mind, and soul to the 5,284 perfect partners who are waiting to meet you right now.

When I counsel men and women in my practice, they often come with a belief system that is sure to lead to disaster. They believe the following:

- I need to find the right person in order to fulfill my life.
- Finding that person is like finding a needle in a haystack.
- Even if I should find them, it probably won't work out.

The truth is this. There are many perfect partners for you. For the purposes of your life, I suggest that there are 5,284. They're not that hard to find. You *will* have to let go of some old beliefs from your dysfunctional love map. For instance, when I met my wife, Carlin, I had to let go of my belief that my "perfect partner" must be younger than me and shorter than me. She is neither, yet we're a good match. What old beliefs do you need to let go of in order to be open to a joyful, healthy relationship?

6. Pursue the Dances of Love.

DANCE #1: ACQUAINTANCESHIP

The dance of acquaintanceship is to recognize that each person we meet is a gift from the universe. We see each person as a jewel to be appreciated without thought of whether they would be useful to us. Instead of screening out everyone except those few we think have "potential," we take in everyone we meet. Acquaintanceship acknowledges and enjoys each person simply because they are a fellow human being.

DANCE #2: COMPANIONSHIP

The dance of companionship is to do what you love to do in the presence of other human beings. People often tell me they go to places to meet people. Yet when I ask them if they enjoy the places they go and things they do, they acknowledge that they do not. If you want to see someone who truly understands the dance of companionship, watch a three year old playing in the sandbox with other children. S/he is ecstatic to be alive, to be playing in the sand, and to be with other boys and girls. In the dance of companionship, who is present is less important than abandoning oneself to the joy of doing.

DANCE #3: FRIENDSHIP

The dance of friendship combines *being* and *doing*. It is an interaction between two people who each want to practice being themselves by doing things together with a partner. Where dance number two can be done with a several partners, the dance of friendship comes in pairs. We often think of friendship as a process of doing for the other person or having them do for us. It is really a process of being with another and enjoying getting closer to ourselves and to them. Friendship is about getting to know ourselves and our partner.

DANCE #4: INTIMATE FRIENDSHIP

The dance of intimate friendship involves exploring the underworld. We begin to recognize in the other, things about ourselves that we don't like or accept. Intimate friends hold up a mirror to each other showing us what has been hidden and forbidden.

Intimate friends often go through times when they don't like each other very well or times when they are inseparable.

The dance of intimate friendship is to reclaim lost parts of ourselves—to re-own our rage, terror, guilt, shame, and also to reclaim our ability to appreciate, accept, nurture, and love ourselves. Intimate friendship is about learning to love and accept the "unacceptable" in ourselves and in the other person.

DANCE #5: SENSUAL FRIENDSHIP

The dance of sensual friendship involves touching. Most of us are touch starved. We never got enough touching as infants, children, adolescents, and adults. Many of us rush into sex looking for the skin contact we never got. Sensual friendship is not a prelude to sex. It is its own dance. In it we relearn to hold hands and rekindle the heat of touching someone we have gotten to know. We caress hair, shoulders, legs, buttocks, knees and toes.

DANCE #6: SEXUAL/CREATIVE LOVERS

The dance of sexual/creative lovers recognizes that the purpose of sex is pleasure, creation and bonding. As we have done with so much else in modern society, we often distill the process of sexuality, and seek only the momentary pleasure. For two million years of human history we sought out sexual partners for pleasure, but also to create children and develop the bond necessary to nurture and raise those children.

Those needs have not changed. Though we may not wish to create children each time we make love, the dance of sexual/creative lovers recognizes that creation is always involved in lovemaking. Each act of love creates a bond with our partner and has the potential to create new life – whether the life is child, a poem, a dance, or an affirmation of the rebirth of the spirit. The dance of sexual/creative lovers continually renews our commitment to life.

DANCE #7: SPIRITUAL/LIFE PARTNERS

The dance of spiritual/life partners recognizes that we cannot truly commit to be with a partner for the rest of our lives until we have gone through the other stages. It knows that the goal of spiritual/life partnership is not happiness, but the spiritual development of each of the partners and the growth of the partnership itself. In this dance, we develop the comfort and security of knowing that the partnership is being held in the embrace of a spiritual presence that teaches each partner how to express and receive ever-deeper experiences of joy and ecstasy.

Pursuing each dance for its own sake allows us to get to know ourselves more deeply while taking the time to get to know a potential partner. It allows us to recognize early on if we're getting involved in an unhealthy relationship. We can either engage the other person in healing before moving on to the next step, or allow the relationship to stay at a lower level of intimacy. Since each dance has its own unique value we don't have to feel pressured to move ahead to the "prize" of finding a life-partner.

Use this space to explore your own questions. What wounds have you experienced growing up? In what ways have you been looking for healing from a partner? Which dances of love have you used? Can you feel good about yourself and your future?

NOTES

Resources

If you'd like more information about my work, I'd enjoy hearing from you. Contact me at: *Jed@MenAlive.com* or visit my websites at *www.MenAlive.com* and *www.TheIrritableMale.com*.

ADDITIONAL RESOURCES:

Black, Jackie. Couples & Money: Cracking the code to ending the #1 conflict in marriage.
http://www.drjackieblack.com/

Cetel, Nancy. Double Menopause: How to Keep Your Romance and Sex Life Alive and Thriving.
New York: Wiley, 2002.
http://www.doublemenopause.com

Farrell, Warren. Why Men Earn More: The Startling Truth Behind the Pay Gap and What Women Can Do About It.
New York: Amacom, 2005.
http://www.WarrenFarrell.com

Gray, John. Why Mars & Venus Collide.
 New York: Harper, 2008.
http://www.marsvenus.com

Gurian, Michael. What Could He Be Thinking: How a Man's Mind Really Works.
 New York: St. Martin's Press, 2003.
http://www.michaelgurian.com

Jones, Karen. Men Are Great: How to Build a Relationship that Brings Out the Best In Both of You.
Boston: The Heart Matters Press, 2007.
http://www.menaregreat.com

Lee, John. The Anger Solution
Philadelphia, Pa: Da Capo Press, 2009.
http://www.johnleebooks.com

Love, Patricia & Stosny, Steven. How to Improve Your Marriage Without Talking About It.
New York: Broadway Books, 2007.
http://www.patlove.com

Maisel, Eric. Brainstorm: Harnessing the Power of Productive Obsessions.
Novato, California: New World Library, 2010.
http://www.ericmaisel.com

Peeke, Pamela. Fit to Live.
New York: Rodale, 2007.
http://www.drpeeke.com

Price, Joan. Better Than I Ever Expected: Straight Talk about Sex After Sixty.
New York: Seal Press, 2006.
http://www.joanprice.com

Stark, Vikki. Runaway Husbands: The Abandoned Wife's Guide to Recovery and Renewal.
Montreal, Québec: Green Light Press, 2010.
http://www.runawayhusbands.com

ZRT Hormone Testing Laboratory
http://www.zrtlab.com

About the Author

Jed Diamond, Ph.D., is an internationally respected leader in the men's health movement. Since its inception in 1992, Dr. Diamond has been on the Board of Advisors of the **Men's Health Network**. He is also a member of the **International Society for the Study of the Aging Male** and serves as a member of the International Scientific Board of the **World Congress on Gender and Men's Health.** He is the only male columnist writing for the **National Association of Baby Boomer Women.** Dr. Diamond has lent his expertise on many of the nation's most popular television programs and most prestigious publications including *CBS, ABC, NBC, and Fox News, Good Morning America, Today Show, CNN-360 with Anderson Cooper,* CNN with Glenn Beck, *The View with Barbara Walters, PBS, New York Times, Wall Street Journal, Newsweek,* and *USA Today.*

Breinigsville, PA USA
19 April 2010
236370BV00002B/2/P